PARKINSON'S

You Must be Joking!

ALONA GOLAN SADAN

Parkinson's? You Must be Joking!
Alona Golan Sadan

Illustrations by Mike Leaf
Translated from the Hebrew by Dalit Shmueli
Contact: alonamatzia@gmail.com

ISBN 9781719819633

PARKINSON'S?

You Must be Joking!

ALONA GOLAN SADAN

CONTENTS

PART I
A PERSONAL STORY OF COPING

Hi, it's Parkinson's!   9

A few laughs with my doctors   13

Meeting on the stairs   23

It's all about choices   27

To C or not to CT   33

The troubles of many   39

Old habits die hard   43

Ninotchka   53

The aliens are here   61

And yet, it moves   69

Down to the mattress   78

Yin and yang   83

The groove of the move   89

Follow the leader   95

A member of the organization   102

Ten GOOD Reasons to get Parkinson's: 114

Black is beautiful   119

Me and my Mannitol   129

A friend in need   135

I have a dream   143

You can't choose your family   149

I like Mike   157

Falling down laughing   165

Thanks for everything   174

PART II
WHAT DO THE EXPERTS SAY?

On Rose-Colored Glasses,
and Coping with an Optimistic View   179

The Key to Life With Parkinson's:
Each Day is a New Challenge   184

Treatment With Nutrition, Herbs,
Supplements, and More   188

Physiotherapy for Parkinson's   195

On the Advantages of Movement   199

On the Wonders of Dance   204

Mind-Body Medicine, Qigong   210

On Mannitol Research and Clinicrowd   215

On U.S Government Benefits
and Insurance   222

Pd Information & Resources   236

Books   237

Important For Patients   239

PART I

A personal story of coping

Hi, it's Parkinson's!

Even if I manage to make this story a little bit amusing, anyone who's been diagnosed with this nasty disease can confirm – it wasn't amusing at first. It also wasn't very funny later on, and I have no idea what the end will look like.

But, hey! Wait a minute. Do completely healthy people have any idea either? So I'm allowing myself to let loose a bit, because it never hurts to make fun of myself or what's happening around me. On the contrary, when I laugh it doesn't hurt.

After years of suffering from this and that, I finally reached a specialist who gave it a name.

Parkinson's Disease.

Somehow, I managed to keep my cool, head held high, straight back. I nodded my head, like the intelligent woman that I believe I am, as if calmly accepting (bizarre, now that I think of it) the verdict. I strode out of the doctor's office with a smile. Even if it was a half-smile, and a little crooked, it was there… It might have been more of a slight lip twitch than a smile…and if I remember correctly I even managed to say thank you, like my mother taught me.

It took exactly five steps, from the doctor's office to the restroom, for my bold bravery and mild-mannered façade to disappear. I lost it, and burst into tears.

I cried for about three days (no, no longer in the restroom), the most horrible images of what I've seen and heard of this disease running through my head.

My spouse, Amatzia, was there for me, quiet and supportive, and I knew that in his mind's eye he was seeing the same visuals that I was; he too was imagining our (not so bright) future. It wasn't easy for him, either.

And then the penny dropped. It hit home.

I have Parkinson's. It won't go away.

I have to learn to cope with the disease, live with it and what it brings into my life, as best as possible. Not let it defeat me.

And with that realization, I managed to pull myself together. A little.

The days to come were devoted to research and reading, learning how I can delay, as much as possible, the progression of this Parkinson's thing that came into our lives.

Now it's always with us; everywhere we go, at home or out, it perches on my shoulder like a parrot on a pirate's shoulder. Or like Edgar Allan Poe's raven, who kept croaking "Nevermore"; it whispers a different "nevermore" into my ear. My own never more.

Never more will I hit the dance floor to rock'n'roll (as if I danced in the past forty years). Never more will I be able to sit on the floor to play with my grandchildren (between you and me – even if I do manage to sit, there's no way I'll be able to get up). And anyway, my oldest grandchild is already 24 years old, has a lovely girlfriend, and I'm sure that getting down on the floor to play with his grandmother is the last thing on his mind. The same goes for my other grandchildren who are already in their teens. I will never climb the Everest (okay, so that wasn't on my agenda for the coming years, either).

I already knew that I couldn't play guitar anymore without my shaking fingers getting entangled in the strings, twisting them up so that all the chords sound like a cat yowling. So I guess more disappointment awaits me, and if Eric Clapton ever performs in our town, he won't invite me onstage to jam with him. But to be honest, that has never happened before, either…

Yet, something good has emerged as I write these lines. I decided to go back to playing the guitar, or the organ. Not in front of an audience (there's a limit to my chutzpah), but to exercise my fingers. And if the sounds I create make some lovesick cats gather round and join me - great. I love cats.

So my big plans are off the table, and clearly my parrot is here to stay, and will make things difficult for me, especially in the most everyday tasks - as a burden and disruption, and a constant presence in all aspects of my, and our, daily life.

Every Parkinson's story is personal; it affects everyone differently, and we are different as individuals. And that's a good thing, because if we were all the same, all the women (how could it be otherwise?), would want Amatzia, which would surely make him very happy. But then – what would *I* do?

Well then, so this is *my* story, and like in every good movie, there has to be a flashback, or maybe even two. Because what do I know? Maybe this book will become a bestseller, and Universal, Columbia, Warner Bros, and Paramount, will all fight over who will produce it.

So here's the first one. And just to say, I will only come to the Oscars if I'm promised that someone will hold the microphone for me, so it won't shoot out of my trembling hand and hit some Hollywood big shot in the head.

A few laughs with my doctors

At my oldest grandson's bar mitzvah, I was asked, like every grandmother who is thought to have a talent for writing, to write and say a few words. In fact, very often, grandmothers with no writing skills at all read a few words they wrote to a round of applause. That's the nature of family love. But we're not here to discuss family love, so moving on…I wrote, I rhymed, and I was invited to read my efforts at the celebration.

I'm used to speaking before an audience. In my many years as a journalist, newspaper editor, and then as manager of the production department of cable television in Israel, I organized many events where I was called up to the stage. I even hosted my own television show.

Even in my other profession, as a tour guide abroad – I never had a problem standing before an audience, holding a mic, and talking (and also singing, unfortunately for the passengers, because the windows on the buses couldn't be opened, and my poor captive audience had no way to escape).

This time was different. I started to read from the

page, and the microphone I held in my hand started hopping and bopping to the Crocodile Rock.

My daughter-in-law hurried up to me, took the swinging microphone out of my hand, and held it up to my mouth, silently letting me know that we were in this together; she would hold the microphone – and I would read. But just then, the page I was reading from began to go crazy, too. Yet somehow, despite everything, mission accomplished.

"It must be nerves," the guests murmured to one another with an understanding and sympathetic smile. And that's what I thought, too. It will pass. And it did. For a while.

However, nothing lasts forever. It didn't happen on a regular basis, but in moments of extreme tiredness, stress, or excitement, the tremors returned and took over my right hand.

My grandson was thirteen years old when the tremors first appeared, and today he's a young man. Yes, that's the grandson who hasn't sat on the floor to play with me for ages.

Don't think that all those years until I was diagnosed with the disease, I sat quietly in the corner shaking to myself. Several more awkward incidents of uncontrollable shaking led me to visit my first neurologist, one of many.

The doctor started the examination with some

neurological tests that I would become very familiar with in the years to come. Look up, follow my finger with your eyes, walk a few steps, cross your legs, a few knocks with a reflex hammer on my knee to check my response. By the way, the little hammer was present in every appointment. Only the doctors changed…

"Did anyone else in your family have tremors?"

"Yes, my mother,"

And the reassuring diagnosis: "You don't have Parkinson's. These pills will stop the shaking. Start gradually, but once you start – do not stop taking them under any circumstances."

She gave me the prescription, and I started taking Clonex (Clonazepam). Clonex? I soon realized that I was clueless - about the side effects. It didn't take long for the headaches to start, dizziness, confusion, and all manner of symptoms. And yet – the tremors continued.

The idea of Clonex made our family doctor dizzy herself. She was horrified, "For god's sake, why did she give you that medication? It's used to treat panic disorders and anxiety in epilepsy patients!"

Well then, if before I had been shaking calmly, now I started to panic – the neurologist had told me that I couldn't stop taking it just like that.

Will Clonex and I be bound from here to eternity, like in a Catholic marriage?

My doctor and I decided that Clonex and I will part as friends, and that I would gradually taper off.

All was right with the world; everything was back to normal, including the occasional tremors.

Two years later, the tremors were stronger and more frequent. Although they were still manageable, I decided it was time to have a few laughs with another neurologist.

The young doctor was short, short-sighted, and short-tempered.

The door to his room was open. I peeked in to see if he was free, and no one was sitting across from him. I saw that he was short when he got up and walked toward me; and as for being short-tempered – he slammed the door shut in my face. I was a centimeter away from needing not just a neurologist, but also a plastic surgeon. But what do I know? Maybe the man's nerves were shaky, but he was still an excellent doctor for nerve disorders?

We started off on the wrong foot. Actually, my right foot was a little shaky. When he finally opened the door, it was the same old routine: "Look up, follow my finger, walk over there, come back, cross your legs," and a few light taps with the hammer on my knee to check my reflexes, but this time with a heavy Russian accent.

"Did anyone else in your family have tremors?"

"Yes, my mother."

"Parkinson's?"

"No. She wasn't diagnosed with Parkinson's."

"You don't have Parkinson's. You have what is called benign tremors."

"Benign? What do you mean benign? Isn't there anything I can take to stop the tremors?"

"Quiet!" he said irritably as he looked at his computer screen, and his impatience level shot up, "I can't concentrate while you talk." He continued to type, slowly, slowly, two fingers tapping on the keyboard, the rest of his fingers lifted like an elderly English lady holding a delicate teacup.

I waited quietly, and slightly shaking, until the doctor finished typing. Who knows if it was from the disease or from fear? Now calmer and more relaxed, he said, "Medications to treat tremors also have bad side effects, worse than the tremors. I think as long as you can stand the shaking, it's better not to take anything."

I don't want side effects. I decided that I could handle the shaking, but after I left his office I kind of wanted to go back, grab the little hammer, and give his knee one good hit. I wondered how high his leg would jump. I can be short-tempered, too.

And so, another year went by. One year older, and still shaking.

It got harder to eat in my usual, polite manner (and

thank you to my parents for my table manners; knife in my right hand, fork in the left). Actually, it started to get harder for me to eat, period. My right hand, the one with the knife, cut the air instead of the food, and my left hand did a great job distributing food everywhere in the room, except where it was supposed to go – my mouth. Oh, and I also discovered one good thing about tremors – when you hold a salt shaker, there's no need to make any effort to shake the salt out. The tremors do the work for you…

I switched the knife to my left hand, and the fork to the right. "Hannah Bavli (Israeli queen of etiquette in the 1940s) must be turning in her grave," I said to Amatzia.

"As she should be," he replied, "that way she won't get bedsores."

But even the switching hands technique didn't work for long.

I started eating using the Thai method. No, not with chopsticks. Even if in my younger years I could eat with chopsticks like a native, there was no chance of that anymore. I'm talking about using a fork to push the food onto a tablespoon and from there - straight to my mouth. The Thai don't need a knife, because Thai food, for the most part, is cut into small pieces.

My unobserved beauty was also affected. After applying eye shadow to my forehead instead of my eyelids, and heavy mascara to my cheeks, I stopped trying to put on makeup (by the way, girls; that problem is easily solved with permanent makeup)

I thought that maybe since the last time I saw the short-tempered doctor, they might have discovered better medication for tremors.

When someone yells at me, the shaking gets worse, but maybe meanwhile some new, young, and enthusiastic doctors have finished their neurology internship. Maybe they are more understanding, and calmer. I decided it was time to go have a few laughs with one of them. I made an appointment.

"Look up, follow my finger with your eyes, walk over there, now cross your legs." Light taps on my knee with the little hammer.

"Did anyone else in your family have tremors?"

"Yes, my mother. But she didn't have Parkinson's."

"You don't have Parkinson's. It's called benign tremors."

Seriously?

This time, the diagnosis came with a little more information, "It's a known phenomenon, called Benign Essential Tremor, and it's hereditary."

Hereditary? This time, I have nothing to thank my parents for…

"Benign, yes, I've heard that already, but what do I do about it?" I pushed him for a solution, "It's getting harder for me to eat, I can't write properly, and my right leg has also started to shake recently," I pleaded, "Isn't there anything, some kind of medication that can stop the shaking?"

"Look," he said, "The drugs on the market today are worse than the tremors. But there are two that I can prescribe with relatively few side effects."

No side effects? I wish…

"They won't be a problem with diabetes?"

He gazed at his computer screen and said, "Yes, they will."

"So what should I do?"

His voice went down an octave, almost to a whisper, "Okay, so if you don't want to take medication that will be harmful for diabetes, and you're afraid of the side effects of other drugs, I have two suggestions. But I'm telling you this off the record…"

"And they are…?"

"Drink wine…"

"I can't," I allowed myself to interrupt, seeing as *he* wasn't short-tempered, "Alcohol is also bad for diabetes."

Not to mention that after reading about the health benefits of drinking red wine, for a while, as is the custom in France and Spain, I drank a glass of red wine every day with lunch. I wandered around the house happily drunk; not smashed, but I would say slightly tipsy.

"And smoke."

I used to be a heavy smoker and quit decades ago. It's a well-known fact that people who quit smoking are more sensitive and annoying than people who have never smoked; they tend to act holier than thou. The smell bothers me even when someone is smoking next to me in an open space. Not to mention the fact that if I start smoking again, it will certainly mean a wave goodbye from Amatzia, who is disgusted by smoking and hasn't smoked a day in his life.

To his credit, the doctor could type fast, but despite his quick fingers, I left his office frustrated, and still shaking.

I started signing letters to my friends, *Yours truly, all shook up, Alona.*

Of course, that was in emails. When I actually wrote something on paper, my handwriting, which used to be big, bold, and clear, became smaller and barely legible, and sometimes even I couldn't read what I had written. But I didn't see any connection between that and my tremors. I thought it was because my hand was getting older. Like me.

They began to appear, slowly. Symptoms that I attributed to the fact that I was no longer eighteen… or twenty, or thirty, or forty. The truth is, slowly but surely, even if it was on shaky legs, I was closing in on seventy.

Meeting on the stairs

I've already drawn you into the story of my life by writing and publishing this book. So I might as well give you another glimpse; yes, prepare yourselves, here comes another flashback.

For more than thirty years, on and off, on vacations from my job as a journalist and later as my sole profession, I was a tour guide. I worked for two of the biggest travel agencies in Israel. My expertise was Spain and Portugal, where I guided summer tours, and Thailand – in the winter.

I traveled with groups of Israelis to these countries and back, until Amatzia, my partner and adulthood sweetheart (I can't call someone I met when I was 49 my childhood sweetheart) retired. We decided that we want to live abroad for a while, and I wanted to continue working. The choice was between Spain and Thailand. We chose Thailand.

I had planned to ask for a meeting with the CEO of the travel agency I worked for, Natour, but I ran into him one day when I came to the offices. He was going up the stairs, and I was going down. Without stopping to think about staircase protocol – who should greet who first, the person going up or the person going down, I blurted, "I want to meet with you in your office, there's something I want to talk with you about."

I was kind of nervous and trembled, not because I already had Parkinson's, but because the CEO was known to be very brusquee, with little patience for small talk, and extremely businesslike.

"Talk!" he ordered, and sat down on the stair.

"Sit," he shot me another order, when he saw I was shocked at his response, and then gestured next to him. I hurried to obey.

My proposal was that I relocate to Thailand, at my expense, and meet the occasional group at Bangkok Airport. My plan was to take the groups on tour and bring them back to the airport; they would return to Israel, and I would return to my apartment in Thailand. I threw him the bait that, "If I'm already there, you have a spare ticket for another traveler…"

"And why at your expense and not mine?" he asked.

"Because if you're paying – I'll have to work around the clock, and if it's at my expense, I'll have time to breathe and do some traveling myself."

"Smart woman," he said, "You convinced me."

He stood and continued up the stairs, and I went on down, to tell Amatzia and start packing.

We started to divide our time between Thailand in

the winter, the tourist season there, and Israel in the summer, with some tours in Spain and Portugal in between.

When it started to get difficult for me (have I mentioned getting older?), I stopped guiding tours, but Thailand had become our second home. We continued to travel for six months every year to spend the winter there. It takes us about two days to find an apartment – and we're settled.

The difficulties that led me to stop working were the stiffness in my body, and the efforts it took to get up after a long period of sitting down, the slowness of movement, and the trembling, which continued to get worse. Did I think it was Parkinson's? No way, it never even occurred to me. Simply signs of age, and better to age trembling than to reach the alternative stage of no movement at all…

And then, one sunny day (of course sunny, Thailand, remember?), both of my hands, my right foot, and my facial muscles lost control. Twitching and trembling for no apparent reason.

As befitting someone living in a Buddhist country, I finally reached enlightenment.

I realized that yes, I am getting older, but twitching legs, uncontrollable shaking in my hands, and facial tics, are not necessarily a part of aging. Those symptoms are beyond benign tremors; they are something more.

I decided that I had to get serious and stop joking around with doctors; I had to find the best.

I googled "hospital neurology departments". This time when we returned home I was determined to consult with a specialist, the head of a hospital neurology department, even if it was a private visit, even if it meant we'd have to sell our car to pay the doctor's bills. If the monk could sell his Ferrari – we could sell our old Renault.

And I still wasn't thinking Parkinson's – because so many doctors had promised me it wasn't.

It's all about choices

Google got me the names of department heads of major hospitals, alongside their photographs. They all had impressive resumes, detailing where they went to school, where they did their internships, their publications, and their clinical experience. And if they were all so smart and so intelligent, how the hell do I choose?

Who knows if and why the head of the neurology department at Sheba Medical Center is better than the head of the department at Beilinson Hospital?

And by the way, my uncle, the late Prof. Jack Braham was one of the pioneers of neurology in the country, but the word "late" is a big clue that he is no longer with us to help me…

Okay. Choosing a specialist.

How do you choose a book? Your decision may be influenced by the cover image, the reviews, the author, and whether you've already read and enjoyed books by that author. Then you open the book, read the first few sentences, and sometimes even the font type and letter size can be a factor. And of course, there's nothing better than recommendations from trustworthy friends with good taste in books.

How do you choose a new car? Okay, a woman might choose according to the color... but women, well, as everyone knows, and as the Duke in Rigoletto sings - "La donna è mobile"; women are fickle. And if you're not really into opera, let's be honest here, even in Judaism, the writings in the Talmud and the teachings of Maimonides don't really show women, and our opinions, too much respect.

We cannot bear witness, and like us, neither can the blind, the deaf, minors, fools, chasers of doves, gamblers with dice, and a few others who can't be trusted.

And as for men? Men, as everyone knows, are rational, intelligent beings and are considered valid witnesses (if they are not one of the above). They will choose according to the model and make, the size of the engine, but they also listen to their friends. There's nothing like friends who know their cars.

But how do you choose a hospital? Let me think... I was hospitalized once and really enjoyed it? My aunt was there for a month and said the food was great?

I did some "email recon" with friends and acquaintances; some worked in the health system, some even taught in medical school, and almost every one of them had a friend or acquaintance with some kind of movement disorder. One name came up very quickly – Professor Nir Giladi, Director of the Neurology Division and head of the Parkinson's and movement disorder unit at Ichilov Hospital.

In addition to the many recommendations, his long and very impressive resume on the hospital's website included extensive experience in Tel Aviv, New York, England, Holland, and China.

And anyway, Amatzia said, "Hey! His father was my teacher on the kibbutz!" A member of Kibbutz Mizra? That certainly says a lot about his character (This, I know from personal experience).

And if that wasn't enough, the man in the photo on the hospital website was not bad looking, and if I have to stand in front of a man who asks me to follow his finger, it's better if he and his finger look good.

Especially when I think about that balance test when the doctor stands behind me, and tries to make me fall backward - because if I have to fall into the arms of a man who isn't Amatzia, he should be handsome, right? However, since I'm not writing the next *50 Shades of Grey* - maybe I should just stop here.

I called to make an appointment, and the earliest was in six months' time. That worked for me, and with our planned date of return to Israel.

So I wanted the best, and reached the best, in a clinic somewhere up on the 20th floor in the tower on Weizmann St. in Tel Aviv.

After waiting a long time in reception, watching people go in and out of the many doctors' rooms, I entered the office of Professor Giladi.

The doctor invited Amatzia and I to sit, and sat down next to us. Behind a big desk, facing a computer screen, sat a young doctor, who typed up everything that the professor said.

Hallelujah! He didn't do the typing himself! My new doctor's attention was wholly on me, with no distractions. How times have changed. I used to associate keys with a piano, and someone playing music - made me happy... Today, I get enthusiastic when the doctor has someone else on the computer keyboard and all the doctor's attention is focused on me.

Here we go again; the same drill and the familiar words. Follow, cross, hammer tap, walk, lift, lower.

"Is there a history of Parkinson's in your family?

"My mother had tremors, but not Parkinson's."

I told him about the other doctors who told me that what I had was called benign tremors. And he, a good and decent man, wasn't quick to dismiss his colleagues' diagnoses. He just explained that perhaps that's what it was then, but that now it certainly looked like Parkinson's. If it walks like a duck, and quacks like a duck, then it must be Parkinson's.

"There's no medication for Parkinson's yet," he continued to depress me, but like the good cop and the bad cop, or maybe Dr. Jekyll and Mr. Hyde, residing in the same body, he was also quick to reassure me, and added, "but we can absolutely slow the progression of the disease, with the medicine I'll prescribe as soon as we get the test results, and with lots of physical exercise."

He went on to talk, straight-faced I might add, about taking brisk half-hour walks five times a week, "and also start lifting weights," he added as the punch line, although he wasn't telling a joke.

Exercise? Moi? Seriously?

"You're in the early stages, and you can live a good life with the disease, even 20 years or more."

A good life? Give up the recliner in front of the television for the gym?

And yet, I did a quick calculation. Twenty years from now, I'll be over 90, and I'd already planned at 85 to start eating all the good stuff that I'm not supposed to eat because of my diabetes.

After years of measured and mindful eating, healthy eating, boring eating (Nothing fried? No sugars? No empty carbs? Lentils? Steamed veggies? Come on!) I plan to wolf down ice cream and cakes, bread and pasta. I told all my friends who love to cook and always have a hard time with the menu when they invite me over for a meal – that soon, very soon, in just a few years' time, they can forget the baked fish and salad, and start making prime rib and potatoes, lasagna, and chocolate mousse, and cake…(I better stop now before I drool all over the keyboard.)

Then, after a few years of bingeing, when my diabetes is out of control, it's *que sera sera*, as Doris Day sang, and as I always say- whatever will be, will be.

But all jokes aside, the fact that I was only in the early stages of the disease, my condition was mild, I had many good years ahead of me, and the monster's progression could be slowed, was no relief.

The doctor sent me for some tests, to confirm his diagnosis. Just to remind you, I left his office calmly - and then fell apart in the restroom.

To C or not to CT

Fortunately, our Health Minister, Rabbi Litzman, decided that the health system is obligated, albeit in his reasoning by Jewish law, to shorten the waiting time for vital tests. A guiding principle of Jewish Law is called *pikuach nefesh*, which basically means that preserving human life overrides almost every religious consideration (including the Sabbath and various coalition crises).

I thought that I'd have to wait six months for a CT scan to examine my brain, but I was pleased to learn that things have changed, and that it would only be a two- week wait. That is, if I was prepared to do it on a Saturday. An Ultra-Orthodox minister made such a decision? He's not Litz-man, he's Super-man!

So Litzman decreed, and instead of sitting in a cafe on a beautiful Saturday morning, we went to do a CT scan.

It was indeed a beautiful day. The results on the piece of paper in my hand said that all is well, and if we ignore my Parkinsonian symptoms, the results didn't show anything to suggest something was wrong or damaged in my brain. Or, in doctor speak - no pathological findings.

Why in the hell do they call it a CT, if they can't *see* Parkinson's with it…

But that was not the last of the glimpses into what was happening my brain, and it was on to the next diagnostic test. This one was much more exciting - Advanced CT!

Onward to PET CT; and here's where things get complicated…

Let's start with the fact that the scan costs 4570 NIS, (the equivalent of around 1300 dollars). And then there's the fact that my health insurance doesn't cover it, nor share in the huge expense. OK, so I don't have to sell my apartment yet, but maybe it's time to start thinking about renting out a room…..Litzman! Where are you when I need you?

But my health is my priority, and although I'm not a Rothschild (Oh, if I were a rich man…), it was clear to us that we would pay the price, whatever the cost.

I called to make an appointment. Before anyone was willing to talk to me and schedule, I was asked to pay. I was happy to discover that even Ichilov Hospital operated under the Buddhist tenets of "here and now".

I read up on the scan. I learned that it wasn't possible to do above a certain level of sugar in the blood – and I got a page of "before" instructions from the hospital.

"If for any reason, it isn't possible to perform the scan," it said, "there is no refund." And it's not because they are greedy, but because as soon as they schedule such a scan, they order the necessary radioactive materials, which they have to pay for.

I also got a call from them with a recorded message. A very courteous and kindly voice explained exactly how to prepare for the scan. I wasn't satisfied with that, so I called to speak to a real flesh and blood person. Because of the diabetes.

A nurse, as courteous and kindly as the recorded message, told me that I shouldn't eat or drink, but to take my medications as usual. I asked to schedule for the early morning, because I knew that an extended fast would raise my blood sugar.

I followed directions and arrived at the hospital on an empty stomach. Before they began to prepare me for the scan, which involves injecting radioactive material into the vein, the nurse asked me if I'd taken any medications this morning. I said yes. "Which ones?" she asked, and I rattled off the list.

It all seemed fine, until I got to Prysoline, prescribed by my doctor just a few days earlier (who told me to start off very gradually). She wasn't familiar with it, and the fact that I only take a small piece, literally a crumb, of one tablet, wasn't good enough.

"I have to consult with the doctor before we can

start," she said.

Okay. So now they have to find a doctor, one who knows what Prysoline is.

An hour passed, and then another. I sat out in the hallway, waiting for them to find the right doctor with the right answer. Meanwhile, I felt my blood sugar elevating. If not from the fast – then from nerves!

After a long wait, I took my nerve-wracked self into the nurses' room. I could already see the four thousand five hundred and seventy shekels going down the drain, and I said to her, "Come on! If I keep waiting here like this without eating, my blood sugar will be too high to do the scan!"

"So why didn't you eat?"

"Because I was told in no uncertain terms that I couldn't!"

"Of course not! Who told you that?"

"Do you think I know the name of the nurse who spoke with me on the phone?"

"There's no need to fast before this scan," she said, and let me munch on the jicama I had in my purse.

At this point, I didn't know whether to laugh or cry, but that wasn't the end of my tribulations. The doctor, who they finally found, said that there was no problem with the medication. The jicama managed to relieve my hunger a bit, the needle was stuck in my vein, the scan performed, and finally, a happy ending.

"Finally! A happy ending!" crowed the parrot on my shoulder, his claws firmly gripping my flesh. Can you call it a happy ending, when the results confirmed the existence of my Parkinson's?

The troubles of many

First we tell my two sons, Eran and Shachar. They actually take the unpleasant news calmly. They ask a few questions, and continue our conversation as usual, on this and that. How are the grandkids, the daughters-in-law, how's work, see you soon and goodbye. No shock, no panic, as if it was nothing. Hey! Hellooo! Your mama got Parkinson's! Maybe show some emotion?! Make your Jewish mother proud?

But I know, or at least hope, that after our talk they'll go straight to the computer or smartphone, google Parkinson's, and learn everything that I already know about this misfortune that's taken hold of me.

Then – we move on to tell our friends. Yes. It was clear to me from the minute I learned of it myself, that I would tell them.

What point was there in hiding or denial? They'd seen me trembling for a few years now, knew that I had difficulty walking, and also that I'd stopped working because of physical difficulties. But I also tell them because that's my nature, because I'm an open person, and I always assume that what happens to me, if it happens, is just plain part of being human.

And mostly, I tell them because I'm not ashamed. I have no reason to be. I didn't steal this "gift" from anyone, and I didn't win this doom and gloom as a prize. And even if I inherited it from my mother, it's a fact that can't be ignored.

Here's where people like to jump on the bandwagon. I quickly discover that almost everyone knows someone – be it a sibling, friend, neighbor, cousin, brother-in-law, grandparent, or even someone who they went to school with 60 years ago in first grade, happened to see them in the street one day and were amazed to learn that they had Parkinson's.

The most amusing were the reactions as if this were a terrible tragedy. The only thing missing was a group of keening women tearing their hair out in grief. Yes, I wanted my nearest and dearest to be aware of my new-old troubles, but I guess it's a matter of degree. Because, hello, I may be parkinsonized, but there's no need to start saying our goodbyes!

Other difficult to swallow reactions were from those friends who tried to make me believe that there is comfort in the troubles of many. Does that make it any more palatable? In this case, the troubles of many are the consolation of fools.

"Oh well, it's not so bad!" say those who try to comfort me, "My grandmother's cousin's been living with it for 30 years!"

Okay. Considering the age I was diagnosed, 30 years is way beyond what I had planned for myself, even before the illness, and I really have no desire to reach that age. And yet, if I remember correctly, the grandmother's cousin he was talking about has been in a wheelchair for the past ten years, with a live-in Filipino caregiver.

"But who wants to spend 30 years with no quality of life?" I reply.

"Try to be optimistic!"

"Meditate!"

"Have you tried acupuncture?"

"You have to think positive thoughts!"

"Keep up positive energies!"

"Remember that every challenge is an opportunity to learn something!" I know, I know, but hey! Why so many lessons?

Suddenly my loved ones find great joy in spouting the wisdom of the Maharishi, proverbs, Buddha, Confucius, and the Dalai Lama.

I know that they are trying to comfort me because they care, and I don't have the heart to tell them that all the stories about their neighbor's cousin, or their cousin's neighbor, sister's friend, or friend's sister, don't help, don't make it easier, and as aggravated as I feel at the moment – they don't really interest me.

Hey guys! This is supposed to encourage me? I wouldn't take you to cheer a lower league badminton team!

Because call me egotistical, I admit right here and now, that if and when my refrigerator or washing machine break down, that will bother me, and at that specific moment, even more so than the repression in North Korea. And my Parkinson's is much closer to me than that of your neighbor. That's just who we are. Kind-hearted beings…

One thing is for sure; just like when I was pregnant with my sons, and suddenly it seemed like the streets were full of pregnant women, and just like when I gave birth – suddenly it seemed like the parks and sidewalks were filled with women with strollers, the same thing is happening now. Suddenly, it's raining men (and women) and they all seem to have Parkinson's.

Old habits die hard

Anxiety grips us; worries about what our future holds are combined with the fear of where the disease will lead us.

Things that have changed in the way I conduct myself that we ignored, have suddenly, clearly, become some of the symptoms, and can no longer be attributed to "a part of growing old."

We talk about our fears, and debate whether to go to psychological counseling. Our friendship and openness, our ability to talk about everything and share our innermost feelings, make us think that isn't necessary for now. We promised one another that when we feel the need for professional help, we won't hesitate to ask for it.

My difficulties force us to prepare for a life that's adapted to the changes I'm going through.

From now on, all the toilet seats in the house are always down. And so that he doesn't forget, I hang a big sign above the toilet, "The seat is down? A thousand thanks! Now when in a hurry – I won't pee in my pants…"

Wonderful! Thanks to Parkinson's I won a battle of the sexes that's been going on for years…

Potentially troublesome mats are moved out of the way, and I state right then and there that I will not get rid of the beautiful floor mats we brought from Thailand. After all, what's a little fall here and there compared to a bathroom with a bathmat that matches the soaps that match the towels?

Another issue is that my voice is getting softer. That's fine when I talk to myself, and that happens to me sometimes because I really enjoy talking to someone who has a wonderful sense of humor such as myself, and the soft voice doesn't bother me. Even without hearing it, I know what I wanted to say.

The problem starts when I try to talk with Amatzia, and my voice is so soft that he doesn't hear me.

"Why aren't you answering me?" I get annoyed, as part of our beautiful friendship.

"Because I didn't hear you!"

"I think you're losing your hearing!"

"And I think that if you want me to hear you, you have to speak up!"

Some might say, "Once I was young, and now I am old. Yet I have never seen the godly abandoned or their children begging for bread." And I say, "Once I was young, and now I am old, and I've never yet met a man who will admit to age-related hearing loss, just like I never met a man who will admit to less than stellar driving skills. (Honestly! I don't mean Amatzia! He's a great driver!)

My fading voice (a proven fact), and his fading hearing (I claim – and he vehemently denies), is a catastrophic combination. I feel like screaming "listen to me" in his ear when he's standing right next to me.

It reminds me of the story about the man who goes to an ear, nose, and throat doctor to ask for a hearing aid for his wife.

"She has to come herself," says the doctor, "a hearing aid has to be fitted personally."

"She's embarrassed and won't admit that she can't hear," replies the man.

The doctor, experienced in such situations, has a solution.

"Go home," he tells the devoted husband, "Stand three meters away from your wife and say something. If she doesn't hear you, get a little closer, stand two meters away, and repeat what you said. If she still doesn't respond, get a little closer. Note the distance from her when she finally hears you, and then we'll know what kind of hearing aid she needs."

The husband goes home, happy with the wonderful suggestion, and finds his wife in the kitchen. He stood three meters behind her and asked in his usual voice, "Honey, when's dinner?" The woman didn't reply. He got a little closer, and stood two meters behind her, "When's dinner?" he asked again. No response. He moved closer, and asked again, "When's dinner?" Nothing. Nada. Totally deaf. He stood up close to her and asked again, and she replied, "I already told you three times! In half an hour!"

We start to worry about what to do if something happens to me in the middle of the night, if we need help, and our children are scattered far across the country.

We decide to consider moving to an assisted living residence.

Amatzia thinks he'd feel more relaxed, with less stress and worry of "what could happen," in assisted living, and he fantasizes about a nice place with dozens of smiling happy elderly people skipping here and there, doing some kind of exercise on the lawn, with a doctor available 24/7, a spacious apartment, surrounded by beautiful gardens, and a well-maintained building with a swimming pool, library, and an abundance of lectures, movies, fascinating activities from drawing to lectures in history, and of course –organized transportation to museums and shows in Tel Aviv.

All right then, we're on a race to find the perfect residence, and very quickly realize that it's an amazing race – to shell out one or two million.

We start our journey through estates, country

homes, and various buildings and private homes that advertise themselves as assisted living residences – where in many cases, the residents need assistance from the owners and caregivers.

As soon as we show interest, the phone call chase begins. We're invited to see shows, to parties, to be impressed by one and to hurry and buy from another. "We have only one apartment available that's just been vacated, and if you don't hurry..."

There's something morbid and unpleasant about the fact that to get a nice apartment, you have to wait for the elderly people living there now to pass on to a better world.

An assisted living residence in a town in the south of Israel took that concept one step further, and built the residence across the street from the local cemetery. That way, the elderly living there can look out the window, and see their next neighborhood every day.

The performances we're invited to are all very nice; from The Gevatron, an Israeli kibbutz folk singers group (I really like them – but I think they should consider signing up for places in assisted living, too), to piano recitals, and lectures. Most of the places we visited were apartments and private homes, on well-kept grounds, surrounded by greenery.

We learn pretty quickly that to live in such a residence in one of the places we would be prepared to or would want to spend the rest of our lives in, we would have to sell our apartment and invest all our money in a small 3-room apartment (small living room, bedroom, and office – as long as we're still functioning, which could be converted into a room for a caregiver, when the time came.)

So far so good, because giving up large apartment for a small apartment is okay, if the assisted living residence is all-inclusive. However, as it turns out, in addition we would have to pay an astronomical monthly rent. Twice, or even three times more than renting a regular apartment.

The property taxes, or utilities, we would pay separately (its different for every residence), and in each one of these places – we'd have to buy or cook meals for ourselves, and the doctor isn't available 24/7. Bottom line, we'd be selling the spacious apartment we live in now to get a small apartment, a few lectures, movies, macramé classes, and bingo evenings.

We realized that as nice and enticing as it may be, it was not economically feasible for us. Amatzia saw an advertisement for an assisted living residence in a not-so- great location. He wanted to see the place. My woman's intuition said it was a waste of time.

"Why trust woman's intuition?" Amatzia asks, quick to protect the stronger sex, "what about men's intuition?"

"There's no such thing as men's intuition!"

"says who?"

"My woman's intuition…" I reply, and go argue with that logic.

However, never mind whose intuition, Amatzia wants to go see, and what Amatzia wants – I go along with.

In a run-down neighborhood, we find a new residential building. I rush right to the restroom at the entrance after the drive. It's neglected and not well maintained; some of the taps don't work, some are dripping – as if to make up for the lack of water in the others. The paint stains on the floor indicate that it's a new building, yet even so, many of the tiles in the bathroom are already broken.

The owner and manager of the place greets us, and his offer sounds great. No need to invest more than one million shekels (300,000 dollars) and the rent is reasonable.

The apartments are so small that the bed is in a niche, with one side against the wall. I'd like to see someone our age climbing up to the inner side of the bed, or crawling out…

"You want a larger apartment? You can rent two, and connect them."

"Swimming pool?" We ask, and we realize we're asking too much.

No. Oh, well actually, "there's a swimming pool

15 minutes' walk from here at the country club," the owner promises.

"Gym?"

"They also have one there."

Doctor? No. Nurse? No. "But if you need – someone here can go buy your medications for you."

A few elderly people sitting in the small lobby follow us with sad eyes, as we leave. It's almost as if they want to go home with us.

In the words of Groucho Marx, "I refuse to join any club that would have me as a member."

We give up on the idea of assisted living, and happily decide to stay in our comfortable, spacious apartment.

We install a panic button. All we have to do is press the button and someone is always on duty to respond, and to send a doctor or ambulance, if necessary. Now we feel much calmer.

Because even if we call ten times a month, and we have to pay even if it's a false alarm, and even if we register to all the possible classes at the community center near our house, and take courses in all the subjects that interest us – we'll still be ahead financially compared to the prices of assisted living residences in places we would choose to live.

And when that day comes, we will get an in-home caregiver - male (if you ask me), or female (if you ask Amatzia).

Another change that this disease brings into our lives is having to give up our winter trips to Thailand. I don't want to be away for too long from my Parkinson's-related activities.

Our group of friends, those who live in Thailand year-round, and those who, like us, spend winters in Chiang Mai, stage a revolt. I forcibly squelch the rebellion. As long as they don't have Parkinson's – they don't have power of veto.

Staying home for the winter means buying a whole new wardrobe of winter clothes. Yay! And we have to get used to heating the apartment because hey, its coooooold here in the winter.

Ninotchka

The sentence, "he helps me around the house," doesn't hold true for us, because we've always done all the household chores, shopping, cleaning and cooking - together. Neither one of us "helps" the other. We are equal partners, and that's true even if he takes charge of dishwashing and window cleaning, and I do the cooking, laundry, and dusting.

And yet, the housework has started to become difficult. I can't bend, lift, or carry, and Amatzia…let's just say, he's no spring chicken either.

At first, I make a mutually beneficial deal with the dust. It won't bother me and I won't bother it. ..

But that doesn't work, and when the windows become opaque, the birds start to nest in the outdoor furniture set, and the weeds start to come up between the cracks in the tiles, (so I'm exaggerating, so what! Give an author the freedom to build the drama!) we realize that it's time to get some help.

I ask for recommendations on our neighborhood Facebook page. One of the neighbors warmly recommends A, and says she is excellent.

Since that was the only response I got to my request, I call her.

Excellent A grumbles over the phone, "My husband and I come over together, and do the job in half the time that it takes one housekeeper," she announces.

To tell you the truth, at "half the time", I already started to get nervous.

Contrary to what she apparently thinks, the 'two for one' deal doesn't thrill me. I can already imagine her "doing a job" on all my objets d'art and knocking them over.

But beggars can't be choosers, and she was my only option, so I schedule an introductory meeting. She'll see if she approves of me and my apartment, and I will see if I approve of her and her "half the time" husband.

I open the door that evening, and I don't see the husband. Not because he didn't show up, but because the young woman was so incredibly fat that she blocked the doorway.

Now it was clear to me why she had to work together with her husband. There was no way this woman could bend or lift herself (not to mention the furniture), clean closets or windows.

Once she squeezes through the door and enters the apartment, her husband was revealed behind her.

He isn't exactly anorexic, but I hope he can do something about the cleaning. Beggars, as I've said…

The two waddle in, we sit down, and after I've already come to terms with the teamwork issue, I ask, "How do I pay your insurance? Two people means paying for both of you."

"You pay just for me," she says.

"And what if something happens to *him* while he's working for me?"

They put their heads together, and find a solution.

"Pay for both of us, and we'll pay you back for one."

She asks who referred her, and I tell her the name.

"Oh!" she says cheerfully, "she's a friend of mine."

And with the knowledge that she'd been recommended by a friend, I'm not so sure if she really works or has ever worked for her, but our health situation, mine and my house, was such that I would agree to anything, as long as someone gets to cleaning the kitchen, the windows, and the balcony.

We agree on a day and time that the dynamic duo will come to work.

That morning, I get up early, and empty the refrigerator and freezer. Soon, very soon, (cue the drumroll) my refrigerator and house will be clean.

I waited half an hour later before I called her.

"I'm sick," she says, and doesn't even try to sound like she has a cold, "I can't come."

I wonder why it didn't occur to her to call me half an hour earlier to tell me the lie and that she wouldn't show up.

I think that she liked my house and me about as much as I liked her, or maybe she's still sick, because I haven't heard from her since.

I spit out a few choice words in a few different languages to sum up what I think about her, and clean the refrigerator myself.

Two days later, Amatzia sees a notice taped to a tree in the neighborhood, with the telephone number of someone looking for housecleaning work.

A warm voice with a heavy Russian accent answers the phone. It takes just a minute or two for me to realize that she doesn't understand everything I'm saying, but it's enough to make an appointment to meet.

Her name is Nina. Ninotchka. In my head, I hear the name in a Russian accent, and it brings to mind the romantic comedy *Ninotchka* starring Greta Garbo.

I heard a story about my wise grandmother, that when she wanted to examine a candidate for the role of housekeeper, she would first invite her to sit and eat.

"Whoever eats quickly - works quickly!" my grandmother used to say.

On the designated day and time, I hear the elevator door open and vigorous steps across the hallway.

Before I even open the door, I give Amatzia a thumbs-up, "Yes!" I cheer, "she sounds very energetic."

At the door stands a young, tall, and strong-looking

woman, with short and tidy hair, nicely dressed, and just a touch of make-up. On her chest hangs a large gold cross.

The first thing she does, after we sit down to chat, is to show me her ID, and with that, I'm completely taken with her. We come to an agreement, and on the designated day she arrives ten minutes early, the sound of her clacking heels filling the hallway.

Ninotchka comes to work dressed and made up exactly as she was for her interview.

"I'm a woman," she declares, "and I have to look like a woman!"

She disappears into the bathroom, and two minutes later comes out wearing comfortable work clothes, and asks, "Where to start?"

I take a look at her long nails and wonder out loud how she can clean with them. Ninotchka laughs. "I use them to clean between the cracks!" she explains, and demonstrates by sticking her finger in the space between the wood frame and glass top of the coffee table.

I go with her from room to room, starting small so that she won't have a panic attack and run away.

In the bedroom I bend over to pick up the area rug, to shake outside. She's quick to scold me, "When I here, you no bend down!"

Ninotchka has been with us for six months now, the

house hasn't been this sparkling clean in a long time.

Once in a while, when she's here, we take a coffee break (no cake!) and chat.

I learn about her life here and in Russia, her Jewish husband who she followed to Israel, and her two daughters, and I'm filled with admiration for her intelligence, and her diligence. It's already clear to me that it's the beginning of a beautiful friendship.

Sometimes I ask her how to say something in Russian; she pronounces it slowly and I write it down. I greet her with *dobroye utro* (good morning) when she arrives, and say *do svidanya* (good bye) when she leaves.

But when I try to teach her new words in Hebrew, she shakes her head no.

"Alonitchka," she laughs, "I understand what you say to me?"

"Yes."

"I clean good?"

"Yes…"

"So why need learn Hebrew??"

The aliens are here

All I had to do now, was to get on board with my doctor's orders; start the medications he prescribed, which I already did, and with the vigorous physical exercise – which I'll get to soon.

In between, as a great believer in alternative medicine; shiatsu, reflexology, tuina, and other bone-breaking and extremity-twisting treatments, I try the alternative possibilities.

Acupuncture.

Only the Chinese, who invented the bonsai and the Japanese who copied that sadistic idea from them, to cut the roots of a tree and force it to remain a dwarf, only people who could come up with the idea of binding and mutilating women's feet so that they could only take tiny steps and not run away from home, or those who invented hara-kiri and kamikaze, could invent and perfect such a treatment.

By the way, regarding the bonsai, today they use a more delicate technique, and stunt the tree's growth with hormones, but you still hear sometimes of some Japanese minister who failed in his duties, went home in shame and committed hara-kiri (in Japan! I said Japan! Not here! Here the MPs never fail in their duties and even if they do – they have no shame, or the honor required for hara-kiri…)

Binding women's feet has long been illegal in China, but they still have Traditional Chinese Medicine, and continue to prick people with needles in the name of medical treatment. Who else would do that?

Which reminds me of a group tour to China that we took that included a visit to a hospital. It was certainly beneficial – for the Chinese.

We gathered in a big room with tables, with a doctor sitting at each one. The members of our group went in turn to sit across from a doctor. Not everyone in the group knew English, so I was asked to sit by one of the doctors and act as translator.

I quickly noticed that according to the Chinese doctor, who acted more like a seasoned horse trader, all the "patients" suffered from the same issues. Kidney or heart problems, as yet undiagnosed but certainly will be manifested in the future, because they were already in early stages. But, never fear! Hope and salvation are yours if you buy the medicine that they (lucky for you!) sell right here at the hospital pharmacy.

This visit was a match made in heaven between the Chinese, who were dying to sell you anything that moved, and the Israelis – who were dying to buy anything, no matter if it moved or not.

I didn't follow-up after the trip to check how many people were cured from their unproven kidney problems, and how many people were cured of a broken heart. Of course, only thanks to the creams and magic pills sold by the Chinese.

But I don't rule out Traditional Chinese Medicine as a whole, and I'm willing to try.

Dr. Mungkala has a clinic in Chiang Mai; she studied both Chinese and Western medicine. I learned that all the foreigners in the city come to her for acupuncture treatments by her experienced hands and pay her a fortune, in Thai terms, around 15 dollars for each treatment.

After I tell her about the trembling (this was before I was diagnosed), she told me to lie down on the bed in the treatment room, and started to prick me with pins.

Then she turned out the light and went to treat another foreigner. It doesn't hurt, and if you lay down calmly in a dark room, it can actually be pleasant, if the mosquitos wouldn't add stings and pricks of their own. Dr. Mungkala is a Buddhist, and a good Buddhist doesn't kill animals, not even mosquitos.

Despite her training in Western medicine, Dr. Mungkala didn't diagnose the Parkinson's, but she did suggest that I start to play with modeling clay. To strengthen my hands.

Like a good obedient patient, I bought some different colored modeling clay, and started to play with it like a three-year-old. I made snakes, balls, and egg baskets, just like in my distant childhood, and with my children and grandchildren. It didn't help the trembling, but it was kind of fun…

I'm also a great believer in healthy eating, and in the curative powers of proper nutrition. I get right on that, also thinking to lose two, maybe three (ok, the truth? – ten) kilos.

After we got home, and after the diagnosis, I went to a dietician. I don't know if there's any nutritional regimen that can help Parkinson's patients, but at the very least I want the other diseases playing hide and seek in my body to chill out, and enable me to deal calmly with this new trouble.

Anat Greenberg, naturopathic practitioner and dietician, sees me in her home office.

She's a very pleasant woman, asks her questions, answers mine, and gives me her advice.

Anat recommends what she recommends, and I'm horrified.

"Are you serious?" I yell, "That's twice as much as I eat today, how am I supposed to lose weight on a diet like that?

Anat laughs, very self-confident, and says, "Give me a month and then we'll talk."

I hope she knows what she's doing.

In less than one month my blood sugar level stabilizes to a point where I can get rid of half the medication I take and the kilograms start to melt away. I have no doubt that the exercise I started at the same time did a lot to contribute. Even so, score one for healthy nutrition!

Amatzia read in some paper about the miraculous healer Oren Zarif. I've known for a long time that there's no good reason to read newspapers in our country, but my husband is easily impressed, and he wants to go to him for a consultation. I object. There's a limit to my belief in what the alternatives can do, to put it mildly.

Then Amatzia says, "Listen! It's not just your disease! It's both of ours, and we're in this together. And if I want to go to check out some treatment, you can't refuse!"

I'm so overwhelmed by that declaration that I'm ready to schedule an appointment with the great Z. Unfortunately, by that I mean Zarif, not Zorro-Banderas.

But before I can schedule an appointment, G.P, a friend of ours, and someone who we hold in high regard, told us about a healer he went to for severe pains he had in the palm of his hand.

When doctors couldn't find a solution and he had

already been scheduled for surgery, he decided to try this healer he'd heard about, who described herself as a medium.

I have no idea what she did and how she did it; she never actually touched him. She sat on the other side of the room, communicating with who knows who, and somehow the problem was completely solved after two visits.

I call the medium. No answer. I try again.

I don't give up, and try again…and again.

When she finally answers, she snaps, "I don't talk on the phone," and hangs up.

I don't get it. I try again, and she says with a touch of hysteria in her voice, "I don't talk on the phone! Send me a text message," and immediately hangs up.

I manage to schedule an appointment by text message, and get directions.

On a busy city street, behind an opaque window that's painted over in white, she greets me.

She looks like an angel, fragile and delicate, wearing white.

Mark Twain said, "Clothes make the man." We wouldn't expect an artist to wear a suit, a doctor to come to work in harem pants and dreadlocks, or for a spiritual person to wear anything but white.

She asks me to take a seat in a soft and pleasant voice, but then she grabs my hands and squeezes, far from gently. She's not so fragile – more Iron Fist than angel.

So here I am, sitting across from her, miserable and in pain (she has a strong grip!) and all the while she's talking to me, and looking over at Amatzia who's sitting next to me. I think to myself, she might be able to cure my Parkinson's, but she'll surely cause my hands to atrophy.

Without letting up on the pressure, or taking her eyes off the handsome man next to me, she says that she can't treat Parkinson's, and adds her insights. Because I'm in a period of weakness, she explains in all seriousness, aliens have taken over my body, and they are causing the illness.

Then, after 10 minutes of extreme pressure on both hands, she lets go, and lays a loving hand on Amatzia's knee.

I feel like yelling, "Hey! Don't touch the merchandise!"

So she can't help me with the Parkinson's, and I have no control, of course, over aliens, and she doesn't talk on the phone because she's very sensitive and afraid of the radiation, and I find that odd, because even E.T. kept trying to phone home. And what's even more interesting, she isn't afraid of committing highway robbery, and she charges us 700 shekels (200 $) without batting an eyelash.

When we leave, Amatzia is totally ready to forget

about going to Oren Zarif.

By the way, in my efforts to include expert opinions and professional recommendations for my book, I also searched for an alien to write a few words about their effect on Parkinson's. However, unfortunately, as I write these words, I still haven't found one.

And yet, it moves

There are a lot of bad things to say about Parkinson's, but you can credit it with one good thing. Without having to give up the car – it got me on my feet, or at least turned me from couch potato, watching television or with a book – to gym rat.

Up until the diagnosis, when the professor recommended I hold back the monster as much as possible with exercise and more exercise and if possible – a little more exercise, the only physical activity I did was the slight movement of my finger on the remote. There's no need for special apparel for that energetic activity.

I admit that I had a great excuse for avoiding any kind of strenuous activity. Take a look at the turtle. Walks slowly, never leaves home, yet lives to be 300-years-old!

I assume that if nature (or God, for that matter) really wanted us to run and jump, we would have been created with a motor, a piston, or springs. Yet here we are – young and old, motor-less.

My active and energetic man goes out every morning - summer, winter, spring and fall, Vivaldi's four

seasons personified, for a walk around our entire neighborhood. If possible he adds in a walk along the beach, and then finishes up with a short swim of 30 or 40 laps at the country club.

Occasionally, pre-trembling, I'd join him for the walk, and then the route would be drastically shorter. I'm hot, I'm cold, it's too hard for me, I have to cook, or embroider a tablecloth, or knit an afghan, plan world peace, and in short, any excuse known to man was acceptable to me, and was met with a snort of contempt by Amatzia.

Country club membership? He realized long ago that paying for me is throwing good money away. Even if I went to the pool with him a few times, determined that this time I'd actually swim a lap or two, after putting my toes in the water my determination evaporated because the water was always too cold, too hot, too wet.

But the good doctor ordered, so I sacrifice my deep-seated belief that sport isn't healthy, and start with the gym.

We've lived in our current house for five years, and I never even peeked into the gym on the ground floor. Now I join, and for a reasonable fee I get a chip that lets me enter the gym that will turn me from a potato – to a noodle.

There are a few plusses to walking on the treadmill.

The room is air-conditioned, no broken sidewalks, no need to detour on to the street, and no chance of stepping on something that the neighborhood dogs left behind and their owners didn't bother to scoop up.

Amatzia continues to take his morning walks outside. He has to feel the sun on his face, and the breeze in what's left of his hair. Amatzia enjoys seeing what's happening in the neighborhood, and if the weather is nice and sunny, maybe even meditate for an hour on the soft sand at the beach.

The difference between us is nothing new. Even on our travels around the world the differences between us are evident.

My man loves what nature created; mountains, valleys, lakes and rivers, and I – what man created; museums, castles, and narrow alleyways in medieval cities. I realized long ago that he and I will never be able, when the time comes, to enjoy lying next to each other in the cemetery. Because he'll want to lie in the sun – and I'll want shade, he'll want a quiet corner, and I'll want to have music and friends, and if he would agree to have music and memorial services, he'd probably want to hear some old kibbutz folk singers, while my choice would be Monty Python's *Always Look on the Bright Side of Life*.

So now he does his thing outside, and I work out at the gym.

At first, I hate every minute. I start with 10 minutes on the treadmill, and gradually work up to higher speeds and longer walks.

I have no patience for the loud television in the gym, and certainly not for the many brain cell-frying commercials. At the beginning of my gym romance, I had some minor issues with one of my neighbors, who pumps up his muscles on the exact same days and at the same hours as I do the treadmill.

I always know when he's there, because I can hear the music that he likes blaring all the way from the lobby. Because he moves from one piece of equipment to the other, the television is on at unnatural decibels, and his cellphone plays other music at the same time, to cover the other side of the room. The man is multi-focal.

"Can you turn it down a little?" I ask.

"This isn't a library," he replies.

I want to say that I know it isn't a library, but It isn't a dance bar either, still, I keep my mouth shut, because his muscles are much bigger than mine.

Weak people have to find ways that don't require strength in the war against those stronger than them. Therefore, I ask him how he's doing, how was his trip abroad, ask how to use the equipment that I'm not familiar with. And lo and behold, within a month, as soon as I walk into the gym, Samson smiles at me, (as if I was his Delilah), shuts off one of the devices, and turns down the other. Score one for the geeks!

In the absence of my only companion in the gym (apparently, the other neighbors work out in the evening), I develop a walking technique for myself that I still haven't registered a patent on.

My technique can only be carried out if I'm alone in the gym, because as soon as other people see what I'm doing, I have no doubt that they'll drag me out in a straitjacket.

Moshe Feldenkrais founded the Feldenkrais Method, and Paula Garbourg, the Paula Method, an exercise technique for control over ring muscles. There's also the popular Pilates, named after Joseph Pilates (I'm telling you this in case you thought it was named after the Pilatus Mountain in Switzerland, or maybe the Roman prefect Pontius Pilate. He's known for the crucifixion of Jesus – but not the exercise method). Now, let me introduce you to the AGS Method (named after its founder – that would be me).

If the treadmill bores you, I invite you to try. The first exercises of my technique are simple, appropriate for anyone. They should be done at your walking pace, and can also be performed while walking and holding on to the treadmill's handrail with both hands.

Move your eyes ten times to each side, as far as you can.

Open your mouth ten times, as if you're pronouncing the vowel sounds: a,e,i,o u. If you're daring, you can actually say them out loud, with the extra benefit of strengthening your vocal cords. Just, please, make sure there's no one else in the room with you…

Stick out your tongue ten times, move your tongue from side to side.

Next, slowly turn your head to the right ten times, and then ten times quickly, all to match your pace.

Now the same to the left.

Tip your head to the right, toward your shoulder, slowly, and then ten times quickly. Then, to the left.

The next stage of the AGS Method is more advanced, and for those with better coordination, because these exercises are with only one hand on the handrail.

Just remember that I didn't provide you with insurance, and there's no ambulance waiting outside. So, if you're not sure about your balance, don't try this, and do me a favor, watch yourselves.

Here goes:

Lift your right shoulder ten times slowly, then quickly. Now your left shoulder. Shoulder rolls, forward and backward, lift your arms – right, left, up, to the side, slow, quick, and so forth.

I make up exercises, and kill two birds with one stone; walk while exercising. And that reminds me of the woman who woke up in the middle of the night and saw her husband on the carpet near the bed doing pushups. She watched him move up and down rhythmically and said, "Why don't you come back to bed and kill two birds with one stone?"

I continue to enrich my gym activity, slowly add some work with light weights, and work out with the different machines to strengthen shoulder muscles, legs, and abs. Just to be clear, there's no need yet to determine that I should lead the Israeli team at the next Olympics opening ceremony.

Slowly, I lose some kilograms, and I can already see that if I continue in this manner, I will become tall, thin, with long blonde hair and green eyes.

And if all else fails, there are other ways to almost become an Angelina Jolie look-alike. Although there's nothing I can do about the height, because I can't wear heels anymore, there's no need to despair. Thin? I'm on my way. Long blond hair? Let it grow and dye it, or buy a wig, and as for the green eyes – colored contact lenses will do the trick.

Even when I was younger, in my long gone days of flexibility, I was never actually a threat to Nadia Comăneci, the Romania gymnast who won an Olympian gold medal at the age of 14. Yet, in my imagination, I complete my walk, and jump off the treadmill executing a perfect Tsukahara vault.

I did say, in my imagination. If I ever do that

gymnastic feat, it will be in my next reincarnation.

I start to walk outdoors. Not the morning walks, because the crooked sidewalks and generous dogs are still out there. But I used to drive any distance, even if only 100 meters away from the house. Now if it's a reasonable distance from home, I prefer to walk. And because I can't walk outside and do my exercises at the same time – I make up rhymes to match my pace as I walk, which is very helpful.

"Remember to take a very long stride; you look like a camel about to hitch a ride."

Or, "You have to walk and clear your mind, but be careful not to fall on your behind."

"Hold your head high – eyes on the street – now's not the time to trip over your feet."

Straighten your back, and swing your arms, walking like a chimp works like a charm."

And so on and so on, as the muse strikes you. Suddenly, walking isn't a chore, and I admit – it's even fun.

I'm no longer a couch potato. I'm a sportato!

Down to the mattress

David Ben Gurion was one of Moshe Feldenkrais' most loyal and famous followers. There's a famous picture of our first prime minister in a headstand, thanks to Feldenkrais. I'm the right age to remember what great publicity that was.

Just one look at that photo and it's clear that Ben Gurion wouldn't stand a chance at getting elected to anything today – not with that bald spot and two tufts of billowing white hair, his soft flabby body and badly-fitting black bathing suit – no way. His squeaky voice would make a crowd break out in wild laughter, and not to mention the way his wife Paula used to embarrass him.

Yet a prime minister doing a headstand is no trivial thing.

If Feldenkrais was good enough to get a prime minister to stand on his head, I guess his technique is good enough to get me to stand on my feet.

I call Miri Gal, a certified Feldenkrais instructor. We chat, and find a day and time that works for both of us. Yes, Amatzia too.

I realize I got it wrong. Feldenkrais did not get anyone on their feet. On the contrary, he lays us down on mattresses, on the floor.

Well, if I knew that there was such a thing as exercising while lying down, I'd be exercising non-stop since I was a child. That's my kind of exercise. I arrange one mattress on top of the other; the princess and the pea has nothing on me. I find a small pillow and do a Parkinsonian flop to a supine position.

Now all I need is my down blanket, let me roll onto my side, and leave me in peace…

I'm surrounded by mattresses. To the right, my man, to the left, some woman, behind me, some guy I don't know and beside him another woman, and soon we'll all start to twist, lift, and release our pelvis. Myself included. This mass lie-down is the closest I'll ever get to participating in an orgy.

Miri says, "Lie on your backs, and listen to your spine. Listen to your shoulder blades. Feel your spine on the mattress, your right shoulder, what your left shoulder telling you…"

I'm new to this and realize that everyone in the room, except for me and Amatzia, are old hands. I do what I'm told, and listen. My spine isn't talking to me. Neither are my shoulder blades. No one is saying out loud what their shoulder blades are telling them. No one is reporting what they hear from their spine. Well, okay, it was a rhetorical question; Miri can't expect a barrage of answers, and I don't say anything, either.

"Go along your spine," Miri continues, "and feel it on the mattress."

How do I "go along my spine," when I'm **lying** on it!

Then comes, "lift your legs, bend your knees, turn your head slowly to the right, then to the left." And the class begins.

Very slowly, gently, a twist here, a pelvic move there, raising arms and lifting knees. There are moments that remind me of a prenatal course, rather than an exercise class. And believe me, that's something that I no longer need, at my age.

Fortunately the entire class is lying down, so I can't compare my lack of flexibility and my moves to the others. I can't see what a klutz I am.

The quiet exercises work muscles and joints that I didn't know I had, and are expressly designed to twist and move each joint in my body, turning me into a well-oiled machine.

During the first class I once again have to deal face-to-face, or face-to-body, with my difficulty performing certain movements. My body is stiff and refuses to cooperate.

A sense of desolation envelops me. I'm battered with difficult thoughts about my body failing me. I lay on my back, motionless, quiet. Instead of lifting my legs to the right and to the left, as Miri instructs in a quiet and pleasant voice, I simply lie there on the mattress, in a room full of strangers, and sob softly.

Miri continues talking as if nothing's wrong, but she stands over me, as she continues calling out instructions into the room, and lays a comforting hand on my shoulder. I pull myself together and calm down, then continue to lift, lower, bend and straighten as best as I can.

The class ends with, "now slowly turn to lie on your left side, and lift yourself to standing." Easier said than done. Turn on to my left side? Easy peasy. I was ready to do that the minute I lay down. But getting up off the floor is another story.

"A chair, a chair, my kingdom for a chair!" I want to shout, so I can lean on something and pull myself up. Miri, even if she hasn't read Shakespeare's Richard III, reads my mind, and brings me a chair. (too bad she wasn't around for king Richard the third…)

After class Miri calls me over. "You know," she says, "I have two students named Alona. To distinguish between you, after our phone conversation, I made a note by your name, 'positive energy'. Try to connect with that."

She has no idea what her words do for me.

I'm a happy person, usually, and I can see the good in many not so great situations. Yes, I have positive energy, and I decide to remember how to reconnect with that, even in difficult moments. Fortunately, I usually succeed.

We've been going to Miri's Feldenkrais classes for a few months now. My movement has slowly improved, and even if I tremble during some of the exercises – I don't give up. I compare my flexibility today (relative…relative…) to those first classes, and see a huge improvement.

Yet even today, when I'm not looking at the clock every five minutes to see when it will be over, my favorite part of every class is what Miri says between each exercise, and at the end of class, "now let go, and relax."

Which proves that it's true that you can't teach an old dog new tricks.

Moshe (Feldenkrais), you are one-of-a-kind!

And then Miri tells us she's opening a qigong group, and we, of course, sign right up.

Yin and yang

If Moshe Feldenkrais gets me down on the floor, here we have yin and yang to get us on our feet and move our bodies into impossible poses.

Yin and yang, Chinese concepts that are well-known in the Western world, are opposites, the two faces of everything; black and white (like in the symbol), light and dark, day and night, happiness and sadness, growth and disintegration, tall and short, life and death, and more and more. Anything that comes to mind works.

Miri plays special music for the practice; Chinese music. If I once thought that all Asian music reminds me of the sound of someone squeezing a cow, not to mention Chinese opera, which is best heard with earplugs, this music is quiet, pleasing, almost meditative.

Nonetheless, we're dealing with something Chinese, so there have to be some harsh tones. The Chinese language, like some other Asian languages, is tonal, and words that to the Western ear sound the same, may mean entirely different things depending on the tone; normal, high, low, upward inflection, or downward.

Another flashback (just a tiny one). I learned many

common words and phrases during our time in Thailand.

My difficulty was in dealing with the tonal language. Because if 'close' and 'far' is the same word, just in a different pitch, how did I dare say to the taxi driver to let me off close to the gas station? And how can I ask the elevator boy at the hotel to get off at the ninth floor, if the words 'rice', 'white, and 'nine' are the same words spoken in different tones? And I'm embarrassed to mention the time I told the waiter, very proud of my grasp of the language, that I "don't eat spicy", and my Thai friend started to laugh, and explained that I had just told him that I don't eat duck…

I once asked a waiter at a restaurant, who spoke some English, how he knew if someone was ordering chicken or egg. He stared at me in astonishment and replied, "what's the problem?" if he wants chicken he asks for kai, and if he wants eggs he says – kai…"

So I went to learn the language, in a special course for foreigners. I thought that if I heard the teacher pronounce the Thai words correctly – I might be able to tell the difference.

Kru (the teacher) Kai (Chicken. I'm serious! That's her name!) waved cards with the symbols of different tones, and asked us to say them out loud. Since in Thailand it's considered impolite to criticize, the choir of baas and moos from the class got us a thumbs up from the teacher and a repeated "good job!" to everyone, despite the chaos in the classroom. Well, how is it possible to teach the accent and correct pronunciation if everyone pronounces differently and the teacher tells everyone they did a 'good job'?

The meaning of the Thai word 'mai' changes depending on the tone; it could mean: no, wood, right? new, burn, or silk. Well, if you can't hear the slight differences in the pitch, how can you say, "New wood doesn't burn, right?" But I digress, and I call myself to order and get back on track:

Because Chinese is the same as Thai in that sense, and the voice accompanying the exercises barks words in different tones and registers words that I assume and check to make sure are Chinese for the numbers from one to ten: yī, èr sān, sì, wǔ, liù, qī, bā, jiǔ, shí.

Miri starts to demonstrate the exercises.

The basis from which we start and return to over and over again is the yang position, which means standing tall with legs straight (A way to remember? Like young people…) and yin, which means standing with legs slightly bent, and a slight curve in the back. The exercises always move between these two poses.

Yang? No problem. I've been standing straight since I was one-year-old. Then Miri gracefully demonstrates yin. I mimic her movements, bend my knees, god help me, who can hold this pose for more than two seconds? (Miri!), I curve my back, push out my behind. I look in the mirror at the front of the room, and I remind myself of a baby who just filled her diaper.

"Put your hands on your hips," Miri prepares us for the next exercise. Hips - no problem, I've always had plenty!

Then we work on balance. Legs slightly apart, torso twists halfway to the right, right hand comes up to shoulder level. Left hand bent at the elbow and palm of the hand by the shoulder. Now turn to the back and look behind your shoulder at the heel of your left foot. My recommendation? Don't try this alone at home.

Or the wonderfully sadistic move where you stand on one leg, raise the other, bend the knee to one side, bend the knee to the other side, raise your knee, straighten your leg forward, move it to the back, with your body leaning forward and back to standing position.

I fumble, I falter, I fake it, and keep leaning on the leg that's supposed to be up in the air at this stage, sneaking a peek to see how the others are coping, and discover that except for Miri, everyone is swaying back and forth like leaves in a storm, and all I can think of right now are the immortal words of Bob Dylan, "The answer my friend, is blowing in the wind...."

If Miri didn't remind us to breathe from time to time, I'd be turning blue by now. And blue is so not my color.

The exercise where we have to stand, hands on bended knees and turn our knees in and out, prepares me for the next time I'll be asked to dance the Charleston at some party (at Gatsby's house, with Robert Redford, I hope...)

In one of the classes, Miri demonstrates a new exercise, and tell us to do a 'gathering' motion. "Imagine that you're gathering up something from the bottom of the sea. What would you like to gather?" She doesn't expect us to answer, and yet Amatzia whispers, "pearls."

My friend Leah, who stretches, bends, twists, and gathers, whispers back, "you have one already!" She's so sweet! She means me...

Someone next to me adds, "But maybe he wants another one?" And I answer them both, "In that case – I would throw away all his pearls and kill him..."

Until the class is over, instead of working to keep my balance and do the moves correctly, gather pearls or whatever from the bottom of the sea, I laugh to myself, imagining Amatzia fluttering, stuck on a necklace between two giant pearls.

We end every exercise with the palms of our hands on the abdomen, over what we call the bellybutton. Miri calls it "laying hands over the dan t'ian". Okaaay, if you say so. After all, Chinese is like Greek to me.

But month after month goes by and I can see my

heel, or at least the general vicinity, when I turn my head, and the "full diaper" look is all but gone. I keep my balance, more or less, and hey, I can even stand for a longer time with my knees bent! A round of applause!

The groove of the move

Amid all the commiseration, words of wisdom, and Confucius quotes I've heard since I've gone public with my diagnosis, I've also gotten some good advice. A friend told me (thank you! thank you!) that she'd heard of dance therapy for Parkinson's.

In my better days, when I was still my old self, I loved to dance, and was the star of every party dancing to Elvis, Cliff Richards, the Platters, Paul Anka, and many others (which just goes to show that I'm an antique).

The only things I have left from my first husband are my two sons (and they are wonderful, if I say so myself, objectively of course, even though they are mine…careful, I'm about to whip out the pictures…) and the last name Golan. He hated to dance, and at parties he'd sit in the corner with the other men and engage in guy talk about the really important things in life, like politics, engines, and soccer.

I soon got tired of inviting all my friend's husbands who still had the energy to get on the dance floor with me, and I started to dance with the girls. When I realized that dancing the tango or a slow dance with a girl was really not the same as dancing the tango or a slow dance with my man, I gave up on it, and became a wallflower myself.

Many years later, Amatzia appeared.

Amatzia loves to dance, and on the kibbutz where he was born and raised he was a star on the dance floor, folk dancing in the open air between the silo and the cowshed. But, unfortunately, there is a big difference between Israeli folk dance and ballroom dancing...

I liked the idea of dance therapy, and once again, I turn to Google. I find a few special movement or dance classes for people with Parkinson's. One with Roni Peled stood out.

Her website gave her professional background, and also mentioned that she had the support of the Israel Parkinson's Organization, that she works with private groups, and with groups at Ichilov Hospital. This means, that my Professor Giladi must also know about her.

We talk and set a time for me to try out one of her movement classes which is located at a Tel Aviv high school.

We arrive on time and hurry toward the building, to look for the classroom. High school students wearing athletic gear pass by us, and ahead of us we see a slim and pretty young woman walking toward us with a smile on her face.

"Hi!" she says.

"Hi!" I reply, and hurry past her to our meeting with Roni.

"Say what you will about kids these days," I say to my man, "there still are some well-mannered young people in this country."

"Alona?" she asks and we stop.

"Roni?!"

I quickly learn that this young-looking woman, pretty and makeup-free, is not so young. She's over thirty, and the mother of a little girl named Doron.

Amatzia and I, who only comes along for the meeting before the first class, sit and chat with Roni, while the others gradually start to show up.

My man is speechless.

He looks stunned at the ravages this disease causes in people, and I can see his anxiety level rising.

Y. waves his arms about uncontrollably, you can't tell a thing about A. until he tries to talk and unidentifiable sounds come out of her mouth. B.'s facial expression is frozen, even when his eyes show that he's trying to smile. H. stumbles into the room, walking on tip toes; R. leans on a walker; M., a serious-looking man with wise eyes and a warm smile, trips at the door; D., who has an amazing sense of humor, limps into the room . I'm the one quietly trembling.

"Maybe joining this class isn't such a great idea for you emotionally," Amatzia expresses his concern on the way home.

And I reply, "It's great for me! Because it's just what I need to make me continue to go to the gym every day, and all the other physical activity that I have to do, without blowing it off, so that I can slow down this disease."

Roni starts every class with a talking circle. Sometimes we only talk about the disease, touching on our fears, how we feel about ourselves and the reactions of people around us. And sometimes, we tell jokes and laugh so hard, that she has to call us to order as if we were kids in school.

I'm amazed every time, at how such a young woman can get us back on track, navigate the meeting, talk about all the subjects she had planned to discuss that day, and add a personal word to each of us. Her kindness, maturity, and experience is empowering and encouraging, even though the youngest of us is twice her age.

Then we stand up and start to move. We start off easy, walking to the beat of Roni's Latin music, shaking our hands, moving our hips from side to side (I've always wanted to do belly dancing. Here's my chance to learn), and it quickly turns into a dance class.

We have a very special camaraderie. The open

discussion about things that some of us don't dare to talk about outside the class, how we help each other, move together, aware of our own and each other's limitations, is heartwarming.

And whoever needs proof of the power of movement as therapy for Parkinson's, just has to see H, so unsteady when she walked in to the room, standing resolutely, and then with a little support from Roni, starts to walk across the room singing as best she can, words she made up to the theme song of "The Bridge on the River Kwai" back when she was a child, to annoy her little sister.

I've heard that the National Institute of Health sends personnel to covertly spy on Parkinson's patients who ask for handicapped benefits. If they see them at one of the many dance classes that have opened recently across the country, like mushrooms after Parkinson's, the spies report that these people are not entitled to benefits – because here's proof – they saw them dancing. So I hope that these spies are reading this chapter, and if it doesn't help, then I hope the earth opens up and swallows them, or some other biblical plague, like what happened to Moses' spies, who were sent to explore the Promised Land and came back to slander it.

I'm not sure that I and my fellow dance class members will start to have picnics together on the weekend, or meet at each other's houses to eat gefillte fish or chicken soup at the Sabbath dinner table, but I certainly feel that I'm part of a group of people, friends, who are becoming very dear to my heart.

Our sessions always end with a support circle. We stand next to each other in a circle, palms of hands touching, and lean on one another, as we sway slightly from side to side. Thank you, and good bye.

Just like my favorite part of the Feldenkrais class is the phrase – let go and relax, this is my least favorite part of our movement class. Because I know it means class is over.

And then Roni tells us she's opening a new class for Parkinsonian's with their partners. Be still, my heart! Ballroom dancing!

I'm ready to follow Roni through fire and water. Well, fire is a bit too hot for me, and water is too cold, but Amatzia and I will be there for the first class on one enchanted evening, ready to dance.

Follow the leader

Like the animals in Noah's ark, two by two, we show up for the first dance class.

Roni's reputation precedes her – as therapist and dance teacher - and we quickly find that our fellow classmates have come from near and far to dance with her.

No heart-to-hearts here, to start the session. Here we put on our dancing shoes (the pros who have them), and it's all about the dance. Just introductions, two or three warm up exercises, and we're off.

The condition of the dancers, who very soon, in just a few weeks, will be dancing the waltz, tango, rhumba, bachata and cha cha to the wand of this tiny magician, is relatively good. So good, in fact, that someone suggested that as part of the introductions we state which one of us is the Parkinsonian – and which one is here because of his wife.

Roni isn't thrilled with the suggestion, because it really doesn't matter. Over time, when we get to know one another, we'll naturally tell each other why we're here. Thanks to which partner we got here, as the dance

lovers will say, or who's to blame for dragging me here once a week, as those who don't might complain.

Roni patiently demonstrates the steps; first without music, then with accompaniment. We start with the tango. She gives the sign when to begin, so that we don't miss the beat. We start with steady steps "forward-forward-forward- side-and close…"

The first few classes are a little wonky. Not just the class – we're wonky, too! Only one or two couples dance with talent and confidence as if they just came off the set of "Dancing with the Stars."

I watch them, women who are no longer slender young girls, yet they dance gracefully, they're flexible, and I'm green with envy. Yes, I used to be able to dance like that, but - too much water under the bridge and my body is dry.

In the next classes, even after we learn a few more dances, we still look at one another embarrassed and confused when Roni says, "and now, let's bachata!" For that matter, it could be merengue or cha cha. Anyone remember the steps? The music sounds familiar – we danced to this last week…how does it go? We stand there open-mouthed and bewildered, as if we have no idea what she's talking about, and we really don't…

A and his partner G are already dancing in front of the big mirror, and with all the right steps! Oh, right, now we remember (no big deal – we saw what **they** were doing). Too bad our memory lasts only until we get home. And don't forget that we're here for the Parkinson's, not the Alzheimer.

Our tough instructor is relentless. She is strict, like the coach of a team of Russian gymnasts training for the Olympics. She insists that we move our hips to the Latin beat just so, and in the waltz, oh the waltz, our hands have to be at the proper level, head up and slightly tilted to the side, back slightly arched and chest up.

This pose, with head held high, and eyes looking up at my man, is precisely the moment I notice that I have to remind him to trim his nose hairs.

And this is also the crisis stage. Not just ours, because Roni insists that the man leads.

The man leads? Why change the world order? That's a good enough excuse to start a world war on all fronts. Most of the men have quietly and submissively been led by their wives for years, and they continue to do so now. They were sure that they came to a dance class, and suddenly they've discovered that it's a lesson in assertiveness and role playing.

At various events I've been to, if I see a man doing weird dance moves, jumping, swinging his hips, doing turns, lifting, bending, etc. while his poor partner gets dragged along on the dance floor, lost and helpless, I know that he thinks he's a great dancer, and that he's making a great impression on everyone watching. But I feel like going up to him and whispering – hey, you know what, despite your magnificent moves and spins, you should take some classes, because you're a lousy dancer!

I believe that a good dancer knows first and foremost to give his dance partner a feeling for how he leads her, and what he plans to do with her. I'm about to spin you around, now I'm twirling you back, now I'm about to bend you backward. Wordlessly, with quiet guidance.

And that's exactly what Roni wants us to do. The men hold their partners with right hand on her left upper back, and with a slight squeeze or change in the other hand's position, to signal the next move.

A few brave men try to take the lead. We hear G. fighting with D., his dominant wife. He wants to lead, because Roni said so, but D. wants to lead as well, because that's what she's used to.

Some women lead their men so quietly and inconspicuously that it looks as if the men are leading. That's how it should be. If you insist on wearing the pants (so to speak) - another woman will wear the jewelry. The jewelry your husband bought her…And yet, a wise person said that the man may be the head, but the woman is the neck that turns it.

From time to time you can hear the desperate voice of a woman, always a woman, chanting the rhythm –

one-two-three, one-two-three, to help the esteemed leader do his job.

And as for my dancer from the fields of Kibbutz Mizra, we really should have introduced ourselves at the outset and state that I was the one with a movement disability. Because anyone who watched at us could mistakenly think that Amatzia was the one with Parkinson's, not me…

He steps on my feet sometimes. I want to say, 'when I was your age I walked on my own two feet," but I never was his age, because he's six years older than me.

Sometimes I step on his foot; oops, sorry. It happens, and then I have no one to blame. A very difficult situation for a woman like me who's always right.

If he remembers where to place his hand on my back, to guide me, he messes up the count, if he remembers the rhythm, he can't decide where he wants to lead me, and if by some miracle there is both rhythm and correct hand placement, for a few minutes – he misses the steps.

Amatzia is frustrated.

"Listen," he suggests, "Let's not tell Roni, and *you* lead…"

A week goes by, then a month, and as the steps become part of the body's memory, we develop nice relationships with the other couples. We greet each other with a smile and even a hug.

Now, we're past the basic steps, there's a new swing to the waltz, and we've added a "New York" to the cha cha (did you know that the same step that's incorporated in several dances, where the partners hold on to each other's waists, and extend a hand out in a graceful wave, is called New York?) The bachata and merengue have become light and easy, and Roni promises that soon, very soon, we'll start with rock-n-roll. So it's true that Elvis was – and still is – my eternal king, but it's also true that my "Jailhouse Rock" isn't what it used to be…and yet, for a moment I feel like I can call out, "Hey younger self…I'm baaaack!"

And then, some enchanted evening , Amatzia leads, and almost gets the rhythm perfectly, and another week goes by, he can signal to me that now he wants us to move sideways, now forward, then back, and we're twirling around without losing the rhythm, and do a New York, and we feel wonderful. We're dancing! Almost ready to sign up for an international ballroom dancing competition.

A member of the organization

I knew about the Israel Parkinson's Organization even before I thought that one day I'd be joining it, because the current CEO of the organization, Ricki N., is a good friend of friends of ours. When I first met her, she was an active volunteer in the organization, because her man is one of us.

The knowledge that she was active in the organization and then was appointed CEO didn't mean much to me as long as I was fortunate enough not to have any idea what it was all about.

However, my day came. I paid the very reasonable annual membership dues – and joined up. And I began to discover what the organization is all about.

I realized that in addition to Ricki, and Amir Carmin, the chairperson who is also one of us, there are dozens of good people; some have Parkinson's and others are partners of Parkinsonians - all of them are volunteers. They organize conferences, courses, lectures, publish the "Parkinton" newsletter twice a year and mail it to our homes.

The newsletter and the meetings with doctors,

scientists, psychologists, physiotherapists, and others who deal in the field, make accessible to the Parkinsonian audience everything that can enrich our insights on living with the disease, and enable us to access more information that can help make our situation easier to deal with.

The social interaction and meeting people who share the same problems, seeing that you're not alone – can also help.

So- are you a member in any organization yet? If not - run (if you can, and if not – at least go as fast as you can), find the organization near you – and sign up!

When I register, I get the name and phone number of the person in charge of the branch in my town, Shalom Hemo.

Hemo, all light and joy and smiles, is happy to accept a new member into the group, and adds me to the WhatsApp group of the Netanya Tremblers.

I start to get messages about various meetings, mostly attempts that don't pan out, to organize a physiotherapy group. It doesn't look like I'll be able to join any kind of activity that this group of fellow friends-in-need organizes. Monday? It's swing with Roni day. Wednesday morning? I stumble along with Miri in qigong, and in the evening – we dance with Roni. Thursday morning I'm on the mat with Miri for Feldenkrais, almost every morning – I go to the gym.

After that, and I have no intention of giving any of it up, there's shopping, cooking, family, trips, friends, and cultural events. I refuse to have my entire life circle around the disease.

I WhatsApp to the group – "Sorry that it won't work out to meet and get to know you, somehow whenever you plan some kind of activity – I'm busy with activities of my own."

Hemo jumps at the chance and immediately replies to suggest, "Why don't you invite us over to your house for a Chanukah party?"

"How many people are we talking about?"

"Around eight."

I get right on it.

On party night, we set out some cakes and a menorah with the right number of candles on the coffee table in our living room. I also add a few plates piled up with jelly donuts, two each and some extra, because if Shalom already informed me in advance that he won't be greedy and will be satisfied with **only** "two- sugarless!", some others might show up just as ravenous, and Amatzia is a generous host and suggests we get some extra, just in case. And good thing we did, because the doorbell rings again and again, and one after the other **20** people wobble in…

The first one in says, "Shalom!" holds out his hand for a handshake, and sits down to wait for the rest.

When the room is filled to overflowing, and whoever was supposed to arrive is already there, I ask, "and where is Shalom Hemo?" It wouldn't be polite to start without the director.

"What do you mean where? I'm here!" says the man who held his hand out and said "Shalom." I thought he was saying "Hi" (in Hebrew), but turns out he was introducing himself!

I'm happy to see the room filled with 20 people instead of 8, but later, when Shalom tells me that he's a math teacher, I hope he's better with numbers in the classroom…

How lucky that I had decided in advance to decline the brick in the gut known as the traditional Chanukah jelly donut. Not because I'm on a diet, but because just like matzo balls, we eat them because they remind us of holidays when we were children, and not because of their sublime taste

If I had wondered how my fellow Parkinsonians would deal with the powdered sugar on the donuts and the sticky jam, with trembling hands and on my white upholstery, I'm happy to say that we got through the refreshment portion with no incidents.

The Chanukah song festival portion of the evening also goes relatively smoothly although, unfortunately, my attempts to get folks to sing a canon in two voices did not go over well. I guess we'll need more than one meeting to work on the singing.

And then – we got to the main entertainment of the evening.

I've come to realize that this will always be an un-avoidable part of every get-together with other Par-kinsonians. We sit in the inevitable circle, and we go clockwise through the same spiel…my name is…I've been sick for …years, and I take…" (this is where each person lists their medications).

Even if someone tries to shift the conversation to a more interesting topic, and talk or discuss something else, there's no chance to chart a new course. Y will always insist on reverting to the topic at hand. In my next get-togethers with the group (yes, there were and will be others), he starts each and every discussion with the same question to each and every one of us, "what medications are you taking?" It seems to me that he gets really upset if someone is taking something that he isn't.

I imagine how after each such a meeting he dashes to his doctor, asking to change his medications. And I feel like giving him a warm hug and saying, "Dear Y., what does it matter? You must have a personal physician who knows you and your specific problems. What are you going to do? Run to him tomorrow and ask him to write you a prescription for the medication that I or B. or G. take, even if I tremble and you just stumble, just because you think that the name of that medication sounds better?"

But no one gave me the authority to rain on anyone's parade, and if that's what makes Y. happy, then I will keep my mouth shut.

Shalom facilitates the meeting; he knows everyone, and when I ask him how long he's been sick, and note that he seems in really good shape, he laughs.

"I don't have Parkinson's!"

"Your wife?"

"Nope!"

He tells me that two years ago, when he retired, he went to the Netanya Municipality and asked where he could volunteer. They told him that they were looking for a tutor to help students prepare for their final exams in mathematics, and for a coordinator for the town's branch of the Parkinson's Organization. They also needed someone to help in community services, as an advisor. What do you choose?

His reply probably was something like, "Wrap it up, I'll take it all!"

When it's my turn to speak, I suggest that in the next meetings, if and when they happen, we do something beyond talking about the disease and medication, and Shalom asks for volunteers to host the next time. There are volunteers.

"If the next evening is also a talking circle around

how long we've been sick and what medications I take, it's the last time I'll be going to one of these events," I inform Amatzia, when we're about to leave the house.

Miriam and Jacob are warm hosts. The table is filled with refreshments that are guest-appropriate – Glatt Kosher. I realize that the group is much larger than the people we hosted. Some of them may not have come because they were uncertain if it was kosher, because there are some couples that I hadn't met at Chanukah. Many of them wear yarmulkes, and two couples, according to their dress, were Orthodox.

The more experience and seniority I gain in Parkinson's, it appears to me that the disease strikes more men than women. But I'm in good company. My brother always used to say that I'm the only "man" he knows.

A.H., a large black yarmulke on his head, gray hair and distinguished white beard, black pants and white shirt, enters the room leaning on "ski poles", and flops down in exhaustion on the chair next to us. Later, when he wants to go to the refreshment table, he turns to Amatzia and asks if he would help him, and my man actually embraces him and lifts him by the armpits.

L., dressed in a similar manner to his friend, tells us in a heavy French accent that he chews gum all the time so people won't notice that his mouth is trembling.

His mouth trembles, but apparently his hands are quite stable. He tells us about the Pétanque club he established in Netanya years ago, and in one of the later get-togethers at his home I see dozens of first-place trophies in Pétanque competitions displayed on the wall of the living room. What's Pétanque? A French game for men. And – no. Not what you might think - N0 sex included…

Whoever has traveled across France through towns and villages must have seen groups of men trying to roll a steel ball as close as they can get to an even smaller ball called a cochonnet ("piglet").

I quickly realized that L has a wonderful sense of humor, so I allow myself to laugh at him and ask, "How does a kosher Jew such as yourself play a game with a piglet?"

He laughs back and replies, "You know why a piglet is called a piglet? Because it wants us to let it remain a pig – not grow up to become a sausage…"

The chairs are arranged in a circle, and we begin. "My name is…I've been sick for …years," and when Y jumps in with "what do you take?" I roll my eyes and look up to the sky, because I'm in the right company and it's exactly the right moment to wonder who's going to be my savior.

I'm about to whisper to Amatzia that as far as I'm concerned, although the night is young, I'm more than ready to go home, when the door opens, and a man wearing a large and colorful yarmulke enters with a guitar in hand.

Miriam, our hostess, smiles at me and says, "I thought about what you said at the meeting at your house, and I noticed that you like to sing, so I invited my cousin to play his guitar especially for you!"

So something good did come from my failure at organizing a choir at Chanukah.

Zackary starts with a medley of religious songs for Sabbath and holidays. Everyone sings, some loudly, some softly, and even though I don't know most of the songs, I happily stamp my feet and clap to the rhythm too.

And then the magic happens.

A.H. again asks someone to help him get up; he and L grasp hands, and dance in a small circle in the center of the room. Joy and emotion fills the hearts of everyone in the room. These two people, holding hands and dancing, could barely walk five minutes ago. Two other men join them. The dancing men are concentrated on their efforts with smiles on their faces, and there's not a dry eye in the room.

"Get up and dance with them!" Amatzia, who knows how I love to dance, urges me.

"Are you crazy? They're not allowed to hold my hand!" I answer quietly, so as not to disrupt the magic in the air. You can't expect my secular kibbutznik to know what is and isn't allowed for ultra-orthodox Jews…

When Zackary and his guitar leave, A.H., who I later learn is from the same farming region where Amatzia grew up on the kibbutz, embraces Amatzia like a long lost friend and starts to reminisce about childhood in the Jezreel Valley. He whispers in his ear that when he was young, he was in a covert, secretive army unit.

However the spy, or Intelligence agent, is not one to remain silent, and he sits down slowly to give a sermon on the weekly Torah portion.

I silently bless our good friend, Uri Ostro, who ages ago was a yeshiva student and today is blatantly secular, like me. Yet for the past several years we've been having our own versions of discussing the weekly Torah portion. He sends me emails with the weekly chapter as it relates to current events, with various commentary and his own interpretation, and I reply with thoughts from my world - – mythology, art, sculpture, and music, as well as other cultures, traditions, and folklore that I've encountered on our travels.

And here I sit, next to a scholar, discussing a Torah chapter. And if that isn't enough to guarantee my place among the Parkinsonians of Netanya, then it must have been when I made everyone sing with me familiar old Israeli folk songs a cappella, after Zack left with his guitar.

Just another word or two (or maybe five or six, but

who's counting) to the IsraeliParkinson's Organization - I have been to a few of your meetings and conferences, and I have a big problem with what happens there. The sandwiches and cakes are always so delicious that I forget everything I ever knew about proper nutrition and carbs and sugar, and eat twice as much (maybe even three times or four, but who's counting..."?) than I should. And so at each meeting, like clockwork when I hit the refreshment table, I recall the wonderful old movie with Susan Hayward, *"I'll cry tomorrow."* I remember… and then stuff my face.

***

When I told the chairperson of the Israel Parkinson's Organization, Amir Carmin, about the book I'm writing, he quickly got the idea, and sent me the following text:

TEN GOOD REASONS
TO GET PARKINSON'S

Recently I've been hearing more and more about a fascinating phenomenon in our region: Parkinson's have been flying off the shelves. People are grabbing Parkinson's like there's no tomorrow. I did some research, and asked around, "What's so special about Parkinson's that's made it so popular?"

I'm happy to tell you that I found some people who deigned to share the secret. I decided to share it with you, so you'll be able to take get at least one good dose of Parkinson's, for you and the family.

So here it is: ten good reasons for each and every one of you to get yourselves some Parkinson's – before it runs out.

Reason # 1: Summer breeze

Parkinson's is a solution for sweating when it's hot. No need for deodorant, or a fan, and certainly not an air conditioner. With Parkinson's, the body creates trembles, excuse me, a continuous wind that blows around you and your dear ones. And just remember – it's free.

Reason #2: Take your time

Strict schedules and Parkinson's don't go together. Life is in constant slow motion. Everything is done slowly. Slowly. Slowly…Wonderful! Now there's justification for always being late and making a grand entrance, just like you always dreamed of.

Reason # 3: Be a badass

(For men only) You always wanted to be a tough guy, a muscled Rambo with a granite jaw. The sphinx-face that you get with Parkinson's makes you look like a real badass; frozen facial muscles, 24/7.

Reason # 4: Disabled permit

You've already had Parkinson's for a while, and now it's time to get your disabled parking permit! Congratulations! What can I say – it's great! Everyone else drives around like crazed cockroaches looking for a parking place in the city, while you get the VIP parking spots.

Reason # 5: Your wife (or husband)

You certainly love your wife. Have your told her that? Brought her flowers? Kissed her feet? Listen bud, it's time to worship her. After all, she's the one you're going to depend on for everything. And I do mean everything…anything you give her now will only be a down payment on what you'll owe her when your Parkinson's gains strength.

Reason # 6: The harmacist

You can see that cute pharmacist every week, even twice a week, if you have enough Parkinson's. Good times!

Reason # 7: Health insurance

As a young man and as an adult, you've always been curious as to what people mean when they talk about (or curse) their health insurance…with Parkinson's, you can finally get to the root of the problem and really understand what's so special about the national health system that everyone loves to hate.

Reason # 8: Significance

Getting Parkinson's means gaining a perspective on life, giving life meaning, understanding how good life used to be.

Reason # 9: Sex

Parkinson's breathes life into the bedroom. No more vibrators. *You* are the vibrator! How can any woman resist?

Reason # 10

If nine reasons aren't enough for you to run and get yourself some Parkinson's, even if it's a fledgling Parkinson's, before it runs out, then apparently you will remain Parkinson-less forever.

Well, gotta run. The line for Parkinson's is getting longer, and I just have to have one.

Black is beautiful

I dragged Amatzia to Europe for our honeymoon; to Portugal – one of my favorite countries. When we got back, he declared, "with the money you're used to spending in a week in Europe – I can travel for two months in Asia. He then dragged me, a sworn Europeologist, to the Eastern part of the world.

When you travel through Europe, see trains, pass by army bases or talk with police officers in uniform, none of that awakens collective memories. But in Germany, even a socks factory surrounded by a fence makes you shudder, and as a Jew, passenger trains give rise to horrific associations. And not to mention that every person you meet who looks over 80 years old, you feel like grabbing by the neck, shaking them and asking "where were you and what did you do during WWII?

And yet, one of the most beautiful places I've ever been to in Europe is the Black Forest region in Germany. Such a beautiful country for a people with such a shameful past.

When you look at the forest, you realize why it's

called the Black Forest, although it's actually green. You can see how the twisted tree trunks and dense forests became the backdrop for Grimm's fairy tales, evil witches who live in candy houses and eat children, wolves who eat grandmothers, and other not so sweet monsters. These are not forests where good little fairies flit around, and certainly not where unicorns can be found.

Once every two years, more or less, I remind Amatzia (it's called nagging…) that I really want to go on a trip to small villages and rivers in the Black Forest, but he was in no hurry. I promise him again and again that I know he'd absolutely love the views and sites.

"We'll do that when we get older," was his repeated reply; my young husband who is closer to 80 than he is to 70, "when we won't have the energy for long flights to Asia."

So this year, the first winter that we aren't going to Thailand because I didn't want to stay away for too long from my doctors, medicines, and therapies – I throw out a tentative suggestion – maybe now's the time for that trip to Germany?

We both know that we should travel and have fun as long as we can, which means, and we don't say this out loud – as long as *I* can. And my man agrees.

We are experienced travelers, and we never take organized tours to places we know we can manage on our own. We've rarely traveled with a group.

So Germany is a cinch for us, and we decide to do it on our own. Also, I've been to this region more than once, and we start to plan a route that includes all the places I think we should visit.

It took a few days of scouring the Internet, maps, and books, before I say to my man, "You know what? I don't feel like navigating, or carrying suitcases, and certainly not walking from parking lots outside of old cities that are car-free, and that also require a lot of walking once you're inside. What do you say to an organized tour?"

As experienced as we are, we know that the itinerary is important, and so is the price, but it's the guide who makes the tour. We find an itinerary that includes all the villages and rivers that are my heart's desire, check the dates, but most of all we read recommendations about the tour guide before we decide on a tour.

How great that we won't have to pack and carry books and maps. Just one new purchase that will join us from now on in our world travels – a walking stick that turns into a little chair.

Two weeks before, Johnny, the guide, call us for a pre-travel brief. Do we have any questions; I have some suggestions; when and where we meet at the airport; and all the procedures that I'm so familiar with from my own tour-guide days.

I have just one question. In the brochure it says that "We will see the Cathedral of..." I know the tricks of the trade, and that "we'll see" means "we'll pass by and glance at them from the outside". The guide will point and say, "This is the cathedral...", and check another one off the list. And if you say, "we'll visit...," that means we'll actually be going inside.

If a daily shower doesn't count, I've never been baptized, and yet I love cathedrals and churches. As opposed to Judaism and Islam, where the rule of *you shall not make for yourself an idol, or any likeness,* is strictly enforced, and with that destroys any possibility of having their own Michelangelos or Leonardos, Christians actually nurture the idea. One thing I can say for this God of the three religions. I forgive him sometimes for a lot of things that were done against humanity, thanks to works of art, paintings, music, and sculpture created over the years, to glorify his name.

For me, cathedrals and churches are treasure troves of art, and I want to know if we will have time to visit some of them. Johnny says that we will enter some of the major ones, "because there are some things you shouldn't miss," and a few more we can go to on our free time.

I decide not to tell him, or anyone else in the group, that I was a tour guide for 35 years, also in the same company he works for, because I don't want him to feel pressured or afraid that I'll be too critical during the trip.

"And there's a P.S.," I tell him, "I have Parkinson's. I don't want any special treatment, I won't ask to sit at the front of the bus, and if you shift the seating arrangements daily – treat us the same as everyone else. I just ask that you note a little **P** beside my name, just so you're aware, in case I have a problem."

At the airport he recognizes Amatzia and me even before we see him. By the time we land in Frankfurt he already knows everyone's name, and we're forty people in the group! I, of course, don't tell him that it would have taken me two days, and a lot of memorization tricks in my notes.

For example, Bella (yes, she is), Frank (he looks very sincere) David (red hair) etc.

We wait to board the bus in two lines by the two doors. We're close to the front of the line at the back door. When it's our turn, I realize the steps are so high that there's no way I can climb up. We go to the front door, and now we're at the back of the line. When we finally get on the bus, the only empty seats are in the back row. I have no problem with that, but I have no doubt that every time we have to get off or on, and everyone will have to wait for me to walk all the way to the front of the bus to get off, they'll have to add a few more days to the trip…

We sit in the back row, when an unidentified man sitting in the front seat calls out, "Alona and Amatzia, come up here."

Johnny asked this man, the first one on the bus, to put his bag on the second seat, and save it for us. Oh to be sweet sixteen again, with a crush on the guide…

So clearly we have a sensitive and caring guide, but – we also have the typical Israeli. And that's something I'm very familiar with from my tour guide days. I know that within a day or two there'll be fighting over who sits in the front, and we have no intention of being involved in World War III. We're prepared to move and sit anywhere, just to avoid the complaints and questions - why first, why last, why she, and why he, why this, and why that.

So here we are, and I'm no longer the guide who always sits in the front seat. We quickly discover that although we didn't sign up for a senior citizen's trip, we're in a geriatric group. Except for Orit and Ohad, who are lovely young people in their late twenties who came with mom Dina, who is just as nice (the apple and tree), most of our fellow tourists are more or less our age, all broken, limping, bruised, and in short, we look like a nursing home tour.

Every time we get off the bus, I grab Amatzia with one hand and my walking stick with the other, and if it weren't for the microphone and earbud in my ear, which helps me to track Johnny in a crowd of locals at the markets and plazas, we would have lost the group right at the start.

Two days into the trip, there isn't one person in the group who hasn't held out a hand to help me get on or off the bus, who hasn't asked if I need help, and our place, the second row on the bus, is saved for us with smiles and kindness that make me feel very emotional.

When we reach public restrooms, I encounter nothing short of a miracle. The line parts like the Red Sea, and everyone motions me to move to the head of the line. Truth? If I wasn't afraid I'd pee in my pants, I'd prefer to wait my turn.

Amatzia claims that it's all because of my personal charm, and the good vibes I create on the bus. But Amatzia is biased. If you'd ask my first husband, I'm not sure he'd give the same interpretation. But me? What do I care? It's my story, and I can write it any way I like, so if someone gives me a compliment…I accept it gladly.

Johnny's just as charming. Between a lecture on the history of Germany and stories about queens and counts, rivers and villages, we compete over who remembers more jokes, and who remembers more songs. All the passengers sing and joke around, as merry as the day is long.

I learn when to pass on a site, and wait for the

group on a bench or in a café. I send Amatzia as our representative, to take photos for me of all the waterfalls and views where you have to climb more than twenty steps. I'm even not embarrassed to sit in one of the wheelchairs at the entrance to gardens in Mainau.

I've learned from experience as a world traveler, even before I was Parkinsonized, that if there are wheelchairs at the entrance to a tourist attraction, there must be a reason, and like the gun on the table in the first act, which almost certainly will be used by the last, so some lazy (like I used to be) tourist, or a feeble (like I am today) tourist, will need a wheelchair that just happens to be right there.

We reach the town of Tübingen, a university town with 25,000 students. The Jews of the town were expelled in the 15th century, and those who returned over the years – were killed in the Holocaust.

Across from City Hall there's a Christian center whose purpose is to ask forgiveness from the Jewish people for what the Germans did to them, and raise awareness of the Holocaust around the world. There is a rich library at the entrance, with books on the Holocaust in several languages. Johnny, second generation Holocaust, invites us to go down to the lower level. I look at the circular stairs and realize that it's not for me. "I'll wait for everyone upstairs," I tell him. Johnny begs me to join the group.

"You know what?" I say to Amatzia, "He cares so much, that for him I'll make the effort."

I crawl slowly down the stairs, leaning on the handrail and Amatzia. Downstairs, in the hall, wait a few young students who tell their family stories, with tears in their eyes. How they begged their grandparents, or great grandparents, to tell them what they did in that war, and confess their war crimes, which had until then been kept as family secrets. And how since they heard their stories, they've been on a journey for forgiveness, and they organize "marches for life" across the world with groups of students, and citizens from Germany and Israel.

It's very emotional, and there's not a dry eye in the hall. When it's over, I go up to Johnny, choking on my tears and say, "thank you for making me come downstairs!"

Two days before the end of the tour, Johnny asks me how we came to live in Thailand. Since we've become friends, and the trip is almost over, I tell him. I reveal that I'm a colleague, and we fall into an embrace like long lost siblings.

On our last hours on the bus, on the way to the airport, when everyone starts to say their goodbyes – stay in touch - and thank you Johnny, an envelope to Johnny and hugs to Johnny – I ask for the microphone.

"I have something tear-jerking to say," I announce,

"get out your handkerchiefs."

I confess that I'm not used to going on an organized tour as a participant. I reveal my little secret, and add, "I learned here that an organized tour isn't for me anymore. I have to travel at my own pace, to rest, to take things easy like people who travel alone or as couples. If I had known how difficult this would be, I wouldn't have gone on this tour. **I'm glad I didn't know**, because it's true that Johnny is great, and Amatzia is amazing, but it's all of you who made this trip wonderful, with your patience, your kind-heartedness, and helping hands!"

And this is where I have to say that Amatzia loved the views, the small towns and gothic alleys, the very polite drivers and the cleanliness, but we were both totally satisfied by two enjoyable things. For him - it was the juicy sausages that he ate in the markets and still recalls with longing. And for me it was the three times I sinned with the famed Black Forest cake (Schwarzwald torte) of the region, with its delicious layers of chocolate, whipped cream, and rich cherry liqueur filling,....and did I mention chocolate and whipped cream?

Me and my Mannitol

A few weeks after I joined Roni's swingers, she invited two emissaries to meet us.

Alon, a fellow Parkinsonian, and Irit Sheffer, who I later learned was from CliniCrowd, a company that's trying to advance and research a magic powder that we will discuss shortly, came bearing a message to the masses of movers and shakers - the discovery of a powdered substance that melts the evil protein alpha synuclein that makes itself at home on the brain of Parkinson's patients, and screws with our dopamine production. And that is Parkinson's in a nutshell. Gotta love that dopamine!

They tell us about researchers from Tel-Aviv University, led by Professor Danny Segal and Professor Ehud Gazit, who discovered a substance that significantly improves the motor function of fruit flies and lab mice after the gene that causes Parkinson's in humans was implanted in them.

In another study, at San Diego University, mice who were "infected" with Parkinson's and then given this magical substance, showed a drastic decrease in alpha synuclein, and they began to move around with joie de vivre, as if they'd never heard of Parkinson's.

Alon is ready to swear that taking Mannitol improved his life beyond recognition. He got his sense of smell back, he moves much more easily, his mood is fantastic, and in short he can join the superheroes.

Losing your sense of smell is not necessarily a disadvantage, in my opinion, especially if your wife tends to burn the food, but I didn't have the chance to ask Alon what his wife's cooking is like.

The good news is that Mannitol, a naturally occurring sugar alcohol in fruit, has been available on the market for many years, at a reasonable price. In the food industry, to be exact, where it's used as a sugar substitute for diabetics, and in candy. It's the white powder you might see on chewing gum.

The bad news is that because the substance is so easily available, no pharmaceutical company is willing to invest in research to complete the process of making into an approved drug for Parkinson's. Why? I'll tell you why – because it's impossible to make money from a substance that's already on the market.

And if you're one of the naïve people who are sure that pharmaceutical companies have the best interests of humanity at heart – wake up!

No one will invest in the research, which means to examine in a laboratory how it affects humans. So there is no production line, and no doctor who can recommend taking Mannitol.

No one is crazy enough to recommend an untried drug just because lab mice and fruit flies started to boogie woogie after they took it, or because someone called Alon, and a few more like him, say that they suddenly can smell again.

I think to myself that if this sweetener is at least equal to, or maybe better than the saccharine sweetener I've been using for years, a product that the FDA has approved the use of as a sugar substitute, then why shouldn't I try it?

Irit gives me the name of a few suppliers (CliniCrowd does not deal in the sale of Mannitol, just in research and advancing it), and I start mannitoling. Gradually.

Alon and Irit talk about the possibility of minor side effects at first that go away within a few days.

Stomach aches? Not me. Diarrhea? Not me…I don't give food up so easily…Gas? Huh, well a refined lady such as I does not pass gas, but to be fair, and in the name of science, I must admit that even if I did, it was not in commercial amounts.

And this makes me think that in the case of passing gas maybe having your sense of smell isn't such a blessing…

I've been taking Mannitol, or as I call it – mannitoling, for almost eight months. I can't tell you if it's doing me any good. When I check my blood sugar levels, or get on the scale at home, I can tell by the ups and downs if my situation has improved or gotten worse.

With Mannitol I didn't get my sense of smell back – because I haven't lost it yet, I'm not sleeping more soundly, because even before the Mannitol I slept just fine, and I haven't stopped falling – because I didn't before, either (knock on wood).

I think that even if I can't see any major changes as a result of using the sweet white powder, at least it's a natural substance and if it doesn't help – it can't do any harm. If there are no significant changes for the good, then the effect is not measurable, and I can't know what my condition would be today without the Mannitol , so why not continue taking it?

I do know that when I started mannitoling and I weighed the daily amount on my kitchen scale, my kitchen counter was covered with white powder. Today I drink lemonade sweetened with Mannitol every morning after the gym, and the counter stays clean. And the coffee I make myself also doesn't spill on the counter anymore, before it reaches my cup.

Over the past months, I've also rallied for the good of science and the public, and filled out the Clini-Crowd questionnaire once a month. The website has gradually become so new and improved, that it's less user-friendly.

I'm not computer savvy. You know, I'm at the age

where people think the computer has something personal against them...

So it's true that I often say to Amatzia that we have to hurry up and have a child who will grow quickly enough to help us deal with the computer, and smartphone, and smart television, but that is also an age issue, and meanwhile our attempts have been unsuccessful.

I've almost given up on the website's refusal to cooperate with me and almost abandon it – when there's a new awakening on the topic.

On December 15, 2016, there was a television item on the news about Parkinson's patients who take Mannitol. One of them was Avihu Ben-Nun, former Israeli Air Force Commander, a charismatic and convincing man who decided, like many others, to try the treatment himself. And like all the other program participants, who saw a halt in the progression of the disease, he attests to a significant improvement in his condition.

And suddenly "my" Mannitol is so popular, that like a little girl who doesn't want to go to sleep while the adults are still awake for fear she'll miss something interesting, I go right back to faithfully filling out the questionnaire. Yes, once a month. Thanks for asking.

Just as I return to the CliniCrowd fold, something mean-spirited out there comes out of hiding and stretches.

Apparently the name Mannitol is derived, totally by chance, I assume, (did anyone else notice?) from the words many and toll, and greedy people see it as a wonderful source for easy money at the expense of Parkinson's patients.

The pimps and parasites go wild.

That really makes me lose it, because a reasonable price for 600 grams of the white powder is around 70 shekels ($ 20) per package. That's how much it was, and remained, at the decent suppliers, those whose greed didn't go to their heads.

And now, after the item on television that showed once limping and decrepit people now running up and down the stairs in their homes, and people suddenly smelling the roses, new Mannitol suppliers are coming out of the woodwork.

It's almost criminal when people who supposedly want to help the sick, advertise "sales" of the substance, for example, one kilogram Mannitol at the "low" price of 329 shekels (almost $100) instead of 473!!! , and urge the sick to hurry... as supplies are limited.

And of course – it includes shipping and handling– so good of them!

If I'd taken high-level mathematics in school I could calculate the huge profit margin (I hope not) that they make at our expense.

A friend in need

Orde Charles Wingate, officer in the British Army, an expert in guerilla warfare, was sent to Palestine as a specialist in Arab affairs. Fortunately for us Israelis, Wingate was an avid supporter of Zionism, and in 1938 he established the Hagana's (Jewish paramilitary organization during the British Mandate) "Special Night Squads."

His service for the benefit of the Zionist movement (in the days when Zionism wasn't considered derogatory), gained him the nickname, "The Friend."

Israel in those days knew how to show appreciation for the kindness of friends. After his death in 1944, when the first center to train teachers in physical education was established, the entrepreneurs decide to call the institute after The Friend.

It's very nice to see that even seventy years later, no one has decided that it's time to forget the friendship, remove his name, and rename it after the head of the institute's uncle or the grandfather of the current donor – as often happens in our country.

The Parkinson's Organization together with Wingate

Institute hold an annual 4- month workshop, in which Parkinsonians come to the Institute once a week, for free, to practice physiotherapy exercises, and beneficial games. And if it's free – you can count me in!

Me and two other Parkinsonians from my hometown Netanya, get picked up once a week by a taxi arranged by the organization, to a class at the Wingate Institute, and back home in the afternoon.

The taxi arrives to pick me up after the others, and I twist and squeeze myself into the back seat. I can't even complain and ask, "is this the way to treat an old lady with Parkinson's?" because everyone in the taxi, except for the driver (I hope), is the same. Parkinsonized.

Between the ride to and from, there's Shachar, Ella, Muhammad, and Ofer. These toned, and insanely flexible (to the point of jealousy and memories of my youth), young people studying at the Institute for certification in physical education, will be our instructors for the workshop. We are their internship. So they have their work cut out for them – to make us athletes for an hour.

The first session starts with a huge disappointment for me.

In the instructions we received, we were asked to bring a hat. I love other women's hats. As for a hat on my own head – it's hot, itchy, and in short – you won't see me at Ascot, and I won't be a source of income for Alice's Mad Hatter. But they did say hat; so I try to obey, and I don't ask why. I find a wide brimmed, bright blue hat at the back of my closet that I bought years ago.

Now I make an effort and find a pair of socks in the same color and even an embroidered bag from India in a matching blue.

We are eight people in the group, with four instructors, and none of them notice that my hat matched my socks which match my bag.

Oh well, I see there's no reward for my efforts, and I wonder if there's any point in continuing to come here...

I quickly discover that in addition to the time and dedication of our quartet of instructors, they are equipped with music from the 60s and 70s, and now I'm prepared to forgive them for everything. It's so much fun to exercise and sing out loud with Elvis, Paul Anka, and The Platters...

The instructors bring out jump ropes. I hope they don't expect me to start jumping. If anyone in our group of eight can jump, I volunteer to sing "one little two little three little Indians,"...and I think that will be the extent of my contribution to skipping.

No grasshoppers in our little group; Jiminy Cricket can go look for friends someplace else, and apparently there is no jumping required. There are other things you can do with jump ropes other than the obvious.

For example, like holding them by the handles to help in an exercise.

The objects change from class to class, and they are testimony to the fact that Wingate has been around for 70 years... the rubber exercise bands that we're supposed to stretch with our legs are as weak and loose as a 70-year-old human body; the band I'm supposed to wrap around my ankles and stretch has seen better days and is now relaxing, hanging slackly around my legs. The effort to keep it from falling off during the exercise is more work than keeping it stretched.

"Stretch the band at chest level," says Ella. We all obey. "Lower!" says Ofer, and I wonder how fast he notices that my chest area really is lower than it used to be....

We switch to playing a relay race with sticks. We do everything in slow motion, because we're all movement-impaired at some level, but we're caught up in the competitive spirit and totter with the sticks in an attempt to beat the other team.

I'm all for the idea of exercising while playing. I may not have had a deprived childhood, as you may think, but I certainly do have a long childhood.

In our first class, the instructors are also a little nervous. "Put your hands on your thighs," says one of them (no names), and to demonstrate, puts his hands on his hips... and that reminds me of the man who happily told his friend about the innocent virgin that he wed, who was so confused on their wedding night that instead of putting the pillow under her head, she put it under her behind.

Our third class is outside; they take us out to the "lawn". What lawn? It's just a small patch of grass. No Natalie wood. No Warren Beatty, and no splendor in the grass, just dry, yellow weeds in the center of what looks like a small amphitheater, down stairs with no handrail, and the way back up to the gym on a sharp incline is enough exercise for the entire week…

K. and D. start to run around the patch of grass, doing a few laps like horses set free, and I wonder if they're in the right group, or if it's my mistake. When they calm down and join the others, the trembling in their hands is proof that we're all in the right place.

"Now you'll go up and down five stairs, and then circle until we reach the next flight of stairs!" says Ofer, and I think, "Now *you* go up the stairs!" But slowly, groaning and complaining, up I go.

Now we're going to play soccer. A scores an own goal, but it really doesn't matter. We all run in all directions, not really succeeding in getting the ball in. No substitutes for Messi or Ronaldo in our crew, but at least we're moving our butts, and very happy.

One of the instructors hears about the time we spend in Thailand. "When you're there, why don't you learn Thai boxing? It's excellent exercise!"

Just the thought of how I would look with those wide boxing shorts, and those big gloves on my hands, jumping around heavily and waving a not-so-quick leg in the air, trying to kick at the head of my dancing opponent, makes me burst into laughter. I have no doubt that my first leg lift would get me down on my back, like a cockroach after being sprayed.

Then one day they decide it was time to really kick our butts, and we spend most of the day working out in the gym, doing interval training with equipment.

We switch every ten minutes from one treadmill to another, from working on knees to working on quads, from chest muscles to shoulders, and it seems to me that it's no coincidence that the Institute's doctor has an office right there in the gym.

It feels like the only people really working out properly in the gym are Shachar, Ella, and Ofer. And also us Parkinsonians a little bit, between groan and sigh.

As for the rest: The timer on my treadmill doesn't work, the speedometer on Shachar's bike bit the dust long ago, the key in A's piece of equipment keeps falling out, and the rest of the equipment is in even worse shape than we are.

But the best exercise of all is when we go down to the main gym and join the rest of the groups, to dance and play different ball games. The Macarena and Lambada have never been choreographed with such sweeping, energetic shaking.

The bleachers in the gym are so low that they were clearly built for strong young adults without knee problems. They could sit on them to during a basketball game or other sport activities.

If the organization's project with Wingate really wants to be considerate of the Parkinsonians that come through its gates, the head of procurement, even before fixing all the equipment in the gym, should equip the gym with benches that are a few centimeters higher than these. Otherwise I and a few other old weaklings like me who can barely seat themselves, will need the help of two strong young men to get up.

I make my opinion known, and I'm happy to see at the next class that there are some "normal" chairs in both gyms.

I wish politicians were so considerate of citizens' needs.

June is coming up, and with it the end of the Wingate workshop.

Beyond the fun and games and laughs with people jumping, running, kicking a ball, exercising, dancing, and running up and down stairs, I also learned lots of physiotherapy exercises through it all, that I can do at home.

So to sum things up, it was great, it was a blast, and all's well that ends well.

I have a dream

We stumble? We fall? We shake? Fantastic, we discovered that we have Parkinson's.

There's an ad on television where people wave their hands expressively, and talk directly to us with a soft voice and sympathetic expression. They promise us, that now that we're lucky enough to be sick, we can sit back and relax. All we have to do is put our faith in them and in Bob Marley, and *every little thing's gonna be alright*. We can wait with our wallets open.

They will take a fortune from us and make sure we get all the government and insurance benefits we're entitled to. How wonderful, there's a chance that we'll get rich from this shitty deal. But not just us.

One conclusion I've drawn from these types of ads – is that acting is a dangerous profession. Every time someone explains how his or her life has changed for the better thanks to the disability benefits lawyer – a caption comes up onscreen saying that this person is an actor.

I quickly realize that there's no need to turn to those TV personalities. The lawyers who handle disability

benefits somehow get the names of their clients' friends and acquaintances that might need their services.

One of them calls us one day and wants to meet us at our house. I explain that from what I've learned, I'm not entitled to anything. He insists, "What do you have to lose? For the price of a cup of coffee, you might end up making a lot of money!" We already see the dollars rolling in, and invite him over. When we open the door, the first thing he says is, "The Brink's truck is on the way!"

Between sips of coffee and bites of cake (which means his visit already cost me more than he said...), he explains that he'll set up a meeting at our house with a social worker, who'll determine my disabilities. If I do exactly what he tells me – he promises us a substantial, steady monthly income thanks to his connections, who have influential connections...and so on.

Sounds wonderful. I already see myself traveling business class from now on...So what do I have to do to win all this wealth?

Well, three days before the visit I have to stop taking my medications, so that the trembling will increase... on the day of the visit I should put a plastic chair in the shower, to show that I can't take a shower standing up, and it would also be great if, in the presence of the social worker, I don't lift my hand up too high, and it would be best if Amatzia shows her how he helps me to sit and stand. If I can also arrange to have a trash can filled with very used adult diapers that would also improve our chances for "happily ever after" - for a hefty percentage of that ever after into his pocket, of course...

I escort him to the door saying: don't call us we'll call you – and I don't intend to. Not to stage a show – or to get back to him.

In any case, I decide that I don't want any favors; I can do it on my own.

I try to understand from websites, friends in the same boat, sudden advisors, what I'm entitled to and what I can do to get all my new benefits. I also have the help of a booklet distributed at one of the Parkinson's Organization conferences.

Because I couldn't make heads or tails of benefits determined by law as they relate to my situation (I wasn't entitled to an income supplement, I'm not disabled under the conditions of National Insurance, I haven't been forced to stop working because of the disease in a place where I'm on payroll with a regular salary coming in) I let myself dream. Joseph could? Martin Luther King could? So can I.

And in my good dreams, I see an exemption from property tax, income tax, a disabled parking permit, supermarket coupons, free entrance to museums, front row middle theater seats (because *that's the way aha aha I like it).*

It's almost like having the childhood song, "Alona and Rock Hudson sitting in a tree, K-I-S-S-I-N-G," come true. By the way, it could have been any other hot guy-of-the-times name in that song, but this is a really stupid dream that has no chance, because Rock Hudson, my love, preferred men.

So it isn't necessary to dream the impossible dream. I'm prepared to settle for a second-tier dream.

In my dream…I don't have to make an effort, or search in books that for the most part don't even deal with situations that apply to my personal needs, and I don't have to run from office to office to find out what I'm entitled to in my condition – which isn't bad, but not particularly good, either…because one fine day, someone will ring the doorbell.

I'm alone at home because Amatzia just went out to the mall near our house, to buy me a present. My wonderful man likes to surprise me with a gift every week, always on a Monday, the day we first met 24 years ago.

I look through the peephole. I see a stranger, a man in a suit and tie and crisp white shirt, wearing glasses, holding a briefcase. Behind him stand a few more people, who I also don't know, and they are all dressed to kill

I know that you can't see all that detail through a

peephole, but what do I care, if it helps me build up the story (or at least, a dream)?

I open the door, and find smiling, happy, and helpful representatives from the tax authority, National Insurance, Ministry of the Interior and Ministry of Health, and a representative from the Bar Association and Department of Transportation…

"We're so sorry that you're sick, but don't worry," says the man standing before me, "we're here to explain everything to you, help you fill out the necessary forms and deal with all the benefits and rights that you're entitled to because of your illness."

"Coffee?" I ask. And I invite them in, but on the way to the kitchen, I notice that the doorbell keeps ringing. It's not the doorbell. It's the alarm clock. I wake up and realize that I haven't gotten out of bed yet.

The worst thing about this story is that the part about Amatzia's weekly gift was also a dream…

You can't choose your family

When I consent to Professor Nir Giladi's offer to participate in Ichilov Hospital's genetic research, I think about my mother.

I inherited many things from her, whether its genetics or upbringing; the same height, hair, which was black in my youth and then turned salt and pepper, brown eyes, a sense of humor, a great love of music, dance, art, literature, and singing.

Did she also pass down this trembling, that she suffered in her later years? The trembling that no one ever tied to Parkinson's?

And then in a flash I think that maybe she did have Parkinson's, and didn't know it? And maybe she **was** diagnosed, but didn't tell me? Huh!

From the level of denial and secrecy I see around me since I started to meet other people with Parkinson's, with the killer combination of Jewish-mother syndrome, I realize that's entirely possible, and wouldn't even surprise me.

And I wonder; will I leave the trembling and other tribulations that Parkinson's brings with it, to my chil-

dren and grandchildren, like an ancient and priceless vase that is passed down for generations, forevermore?

So I'm all for volunteering my body to science – but it depends on how much they intend to prick and prod me for the purpose of their research.

Before I meet the prickers and prodders at Ichilov, I get an email with forms that I have to fill out.

The first form is so hard to read, with small letters and so little space that clearly the person who typed it has no knowledge of Parkinson's. How can I write anything on these lines, when my Parkinsonized handwriting, tiny and crooked as it is, needs some breathing room to express itself properly?

Never mind, I'll manage, and whoever has to read my hieroglyphics – good luck to them!

The next page is full of invasive questions.

I love quizzes and crossword puzzles, and I'm ready to tackle forms, as long as they're not for income tax. I happily dig into the multiple choice form.

Do I have feelings of guilt? All the time? Most of the time? Not particularly?

We've already established my "Jewish mother" tendencies, so of course I have feelings of guilt. Too bad they don't ask if someone else is guiltier than me…

Questions like: Are there a lot of things that **don't** bother you? None/barely/a little/very - make me feel like I'm being asked trick questions.

I'm asked about my drinking habits, smoking habits, and even about my sex life. If that were an acronym for Shopping – Exercise – X-rays - okay, I can answer that. But if not – who remembers?

They schedule an appointment at the Genetics Institute at Ichilov, and tell me to bring the full questionnaire and lots of patience, because it will take at least three hours. And also my bank account number. These nice people are actually paying me for my contribution to science!

An explanation by a geneticist on the hows and whys and who it's good for, neurological exams, lift, lower – follow my finger with your eyes – and the familiar little hammer. I recall the Mike Leaf caricature with the hammer and burst out laughing. The astonished neurologist is used to patients who are more polite and reserved than me.

Blood work? No biggie; I donated blood for years until they decided I was too old and didn't need any favors from me.

I'm asked to fill a cup for a urine test. Finally, someone appreciates and even asks to examine the copious amounts I produce! Mission accomplished. I could even donate to other patients, if necessary.

When all my Parkinsonized acquaintances told me that the first thing they lost was their sense of smell, I could boast that mine was intact, although I have no ideas what there is to boast about. And here, it's put to the test. I get little booklets with brown squares at the bottom of each page (Brown? Does that mean I get to smell poop?) that I have to scratch and sniff, and choose which of four possible smells it reminds me of.

Pineapple, strawberry, smoke, gasoline, roses, and other more or less pleasant smells waft up to my nose.

I pass the smell test with flying colors (straight to flight school – right?) although as someone who doesn't drink alcohol I surely failed the whisky smell test, and as someone who doesn't eat dairy, I'm not sure I identified the cheddar.

We play some more games. Yay! Next up is word games!

The examiner holds up little drawings of disassembled objects, and I have to identify them.

I'm asked to count all the fruits and vegetables I know, and all the animals I know, in a timed test. Like Scattergories. I love that game, and I was always good at it, no matter the letter or category (Who can prove that knuckle isn't a kind of sandwich!).

But when it comes to types of cars – my list is much shorter. Oh, so now it's a game for men?

As many words for a certain letter as I can on a timer, and then for another letter.

They read me a list of words. A short list, then a long one. I won't give you the list here, so as not to ruin things for the Genetics Institute.

Memorizing the short list is no problem, thanks to our friend Eran Katz, who holds the Israeli Guinness Book of World Records title in memory stunts, and teaches memory boosting techniques in his lectures and books.

With just a short glance at a board with 500 random-ly-written numbers called out from the audience, Eran memorizes them all and can read them out from first to last and last to first, so what's so hard about a nine-word list for someone who's learned his technique?

As for the longer list, which I'm asked to recite after we went on to an entirely different topic, Eran's method doesn't really work for me. I guess, after all, you have to hold a Guinness world record for that....

The need to succeed in these tests, with no score and no certificate, whose purpose is just to determine mo-tor function, cognitive, and health status, is probably embedded deep inside us, and part of our nature. Why is it so important to me to prove to these researchers that I can memorize more words than I actually can? Chalk it up to human nature.

With all my love of word games, when we reach the "numbers game", I get stuck. My brain, which I am proud to call sharp-witted and quick, is sealed off with gray film and shuts down. Gray is the new blackout.

Subtract multiples of seven from a number in the

hundreds? Why seven? Five would be so much easier.

If all the punishments I got for not learning the multiplication table by heart when I was a child didn't work –a genetic test will?

And to do it while walking quickly back and forth along a corridor while being timed with a stopper?

Okay, I think to myself, so you wouldn't be recruited to the Air Force as a cadet, maybe only as a mechanic.

I like Mike

A few months ago, I woke up in the middle of the night and started writing this story.

Over the years, I've written a few books in my head; I've imagined starts, middles, and endings. But this awakening with the urge to sit down and write wasn't like those other books, and they are still in the desk drawer. It was clear to me that this need to get up and write in the middle of the night would go through to the end and get published, just like in my previous book, "Empty Envelopes," which was published five years ago, and also started writing itself in the middle of the night.

At night I already saw the entire structure of the book in my head, and I hurried to the computer to get it all down.

One thing was clear to me from the start; it wasn't going to be a "woe is me, why did this happen to me" kind of book. Rather, it would be more in line with my nature – optimistic and with a touch of humor.

I also had the illustrations outlined in my head, and I knew they matched the text I intended to write. I also knew who would draw them – Mike Leaf.

I was overjoyed when Mike gladly accepted, and immediately started on the project.

In 2000, when we lived in Chiang Mai, the lovely N.K. contacted us. She had traveled to Thailand a year earlier in one of my groups, and told us that good friends of hers, a couple, also wanted to come to live in Chiang Mai for a few months. Could she give them our phone number? Could we help them?

We are pro-immigration, even if it's to Thailand, so of course we said yes.

After a trans-Atlantic call with Rachel Leaf, his significant other, we promised to get them an apartment next to us, and pick them up from the airport.

We made a big sign with the name Leaf, and I drew a big colorful leaf on it (in case they couldn't read), and on the day they were supposed to arrive, we waited for them at the airport. I had no idea what they looked like, but the sign was big enough and clear enough for anyone with two eyes in his head to see.

The plane landed, passengers came out, the arrival hall emptied, and we stopped waving the sign because there was no one left to see it. Had the Leafs passed us without noticing?

Just as we were about to leave and go back home, a tall man with an angry look in his eyes and a sparse beard, stormed into the arrivals hall. The first two sentences he said to us, in a strong British accent, were, "these f**king motherf***ers lost our suitcases!" and "Where can I get some good stuff to smoke?"

We couldn't help much with the suitcase (which arrived the next day), and we didn't know where to get any "good stuff" (but Mike is a resourceful guy, so we discovered), and yet, despite these two total failures when we first met, we clicked immediately.

I suspect that Mike liked me and us, at first because (or thanks to?) the fact that it was nice for him to meet someone who, like him, isn't always politically correct in her use of language. Rachel, very gentle and reserved, is the complete opposite of wild man Mike, and she still blushes at his blunt language even after 48 years together. And as for Amatzia, who is also sometimes shocked at my language, it's impossible not to love him anyway!

Over the 17 years of friendship across oceans and continents, every winter in Thailand and summer in Israel, we learned that Mike's life story, and his artistic talents, justify a book of its own.

Mike was born in London in 1934. During WWII, when he was five-years-old, he lived with his uncle, who had a store for kitchen tools and accessories.

While bombs were falling on London, and German Messerschmitts and British Spitfires battled in the skies, his uncle hid him in a big trashcan that was for sale in his store. "Ever since," Mike says in a mix of Hebrew and English, "I've been drawn to shit and garbage, and maybe that's why I like to deal with them and sculpt with paper mache from old newspapers."

When he was 17, before he made Aliyah to Israel, he wanted to see the world. At that time his parents were living in South Africa, and he missed them, but didn't have the money to fly there. That fit in beautifully with his spirit of adventure. Mike set out on a journey that started on a ferry and continued with hitchhiking and on foot, from England to South Africa. On his way he met people and tribes that he didn't know, he says, whether they were going to help him – or eat him.

One day, he saw in the distance a man coming his way. He didn't have the fluid gait that Mike had come to identify with the natives, but was rather stiff and military-like. When they got closer to each other, Mike saw that he had been right in a way. The man apparently had served in the past in the British Army, and was wearing a threadbare uniform. He stood facing Mike, clicked his heels together, straightened his back, saluted and asked, "And How is Her Majesty, Queen Elizabeth?" When Mike answered, "Fine, thank you, and how are you?" he was rewarded with a fascinating evening and an invitation to the tribe's campfire.

Mike made Aliyah and joined Kibbutz Amiad in the north, "I continued with my childhood love of garbage, and shoveled shit in the cowshed."

Mike volunteered to serve in the IDF's first para-trooper unit. He participated in the Sinai War and was badly wounded in the battle at Mitla Pass. When he saw that the kibbutz was too considerate of his disability from his injury and didn't let him do any hard physical labor, he realized that his only chance to properly recover was to drive himself to work hard – and so he left the kibbutz.

Mike traveled the world, worked on cattle ranches in Africa, and other farming jobs in England. He felt himself getting stronger.

He returned to Israel, and while wandering around in the old city of Safed, he came across the ruins of an old house. He fixed it up stone after stone, cleared away piles of dirt and debris, and built with his two hands what would become his home with Rachel for many years.

Leaf says that he loves to recharge his batteries by getting to know new cultures, so he and Rachel traveled around the world. Twice they went on a year-long trip in an improvised caravan that Mike built himself, and traveled through Europe and South Africa, earning their living from selling Mike's art.

They wandered and lived, for six months at a time, in Mexico, the U.S., Indonesia, India, Morocco, Greece, and various countries in Africa, gathering experiences and friends, because no one can resist their charm.

Following Mike's decision to devote himself to his art, the Leafs opened an art gallery in Safed's artist quarter. Rachel, ever practical, was responsible for sales, and absentminded Mike – for the art. A few years ago they had to close their successful gallery, due to the increasingly Orthodox nature of the city, which was followed by a decrease in tourism.

Mike's works were exhibited in Israel, England, Mexico, and the United States, gained recognition and admiration, and he was even awarded a scholarship in the U.S. by The Pollock-Krasner Foundation.

Mike's work is very diverse. He draws, sculpts, illustrates, and writes short stories in English – he's already published four books. His paper mache works are full of humor, just like his books, and like the man himself.

His medical condition deteriorated over the years as a result of his old injury, and his advanced age (do the math…), and he's not allowed to go on wild adventures around the world anymore. He's content with spending six months in Israel, and six months in Thailand, which is a very user-friendly country. Their first trip to Thailand brought them to us, and since then they've been going back and forth with us every year.

It's difficult for Mike to walk these days, but he insists on walking the streets in Chiang Mai with a cane. On one of his walks in town he met a man whose arms had been amputated, who was whizzing by on skates.

"Hey!" Mike smiled at him, "give me a piggy-back ride and together we'll be a whole person. We'll use your legs and my hands!" The man laughed, stopped to chat, and then for a beer, and Mike had made another new friend.

And by the way, Mikey, if you meant for the nice old lady in your illustrations to look like me, then look again.

Yes, the face is similar, but I'm much taller, thinner, and even if my boobs aren't exactly where they once were – still, they aren't that big and droopy. But what can I say, when I see how Picasso drew women, I'm willing to forgive you...

Falling down laughing

My story is coming to an end.

I haven't gotten rid of the Parkinson's, but I have made peace with it – and for now – that's my story. I still don't know what I'll be keeping myself busy with in the days to come. I don't think it will be accompanying anyone on my guitar, or jewelry making, and walking the tightrope in the circus is off the table.

But I have and always will have family, good friends, and interesting people to meet, and thousands of books I haven't read yet, and operas to see again and again, and artists will continue to write plays and music, and create and direct movies and new shows, there will always be places in the world to visit and revisit, and there's the next season of "Game of Thrones" … so there are certainly plenty of good things to look forward to. (Well, good if George R. R. Martin doesn't kill Tyrion Lanister and Jon Snow…)

I'm sure that there are also many activities going on in your towns and cities, and if you're looking for something that suits you, you will find them, because these spring up like mushrooms after Parkinson's.

I haven't tried aqua therapy because the water is usually too cold for me, and now is the time and place to quote my aunt, who loved to tan at the municipal pool in Tel-Aviv, but never dipped in the water or swam. When she was asked why she never went into the water, she'd say, "because I don't know how to swim, and I don't need to pee."

I haven't taken voice lessons, because I have no need for them, and I fear that the minute I start and try to do my homework – I'll be the cause of a significant decrease in the price of apartments in our neighborhood. That, of course, is not something I want to happen...

What I would like to happen, is to be able to continue to joke around with our grandchildren and enjoy their creative thinking, and the new activities that they suggest to get the most out of my Parkinson's.

Rom, who built an iRom-bot by connecting an old printer motor to a broom, claims that he can attach a broom to me and then I can move around the house and sweep as I go with the force of my trembling alone.

Yiftah said he could easily find me a job at a cocktail bar, because I'd be great with a shaker, and Nadav thinks it would be easy and convenient for me to hold a fan in the summer, because I wouldn't have to make an effort to wave it.

Yes, I have Parkinson's, and yes, my life is good.

I have Parkinson's, and I'm not ashamed of it. I didn't steal it, and didn't sin for it. Believe me when I say that instead I would have preferred to receive a case of pink champagne or chocolate from a generous benefactor.

As far as I know, I didn't do something terrible in my previous incarnation, or the one before, that I had to pay for with this "gift".

And yet, it's here. And when I see a person I know who isn't aware, or a stranger who looks inquisitively at my shaking right hand, I smile and say, "I have Parkinson's."

I discover that my openness – encourages openness. Suddenly, I understand that I am a messenger (and they say don't shoot the messenger...) because with the number of people who opened their hearts to me, and told me in confidence that they, too, suffered from tremors, that they're afraid to go to the doctor, and I convinced them so that they wouldn't delay treatment if they needed it, and the number of people I told about the activities of the organization who signed up for them, and the people I dragged with me to qigong or Roni's classes – it seems to me that I've earned myself a good place (not further than row 10 in the middle, in the orchestra!) in Heaven.

Not everyone trembles and falls, and not everyone is Parkinsonized. In most cases, people's response is simply to show their willingness to help if necessary, and the amount of good will I've encountered in such cases moves me to tears.

Friends from the Parkinson's world tell me that it took years for them to find the courage to tell their families about the disease. Many don't talk about it among their friends, or at work. And I wonder. Do you really think no one notices your trembling hand? Don't notice that you're gradually losing your voice, or that your walk has changed? How naïve and in denial can you be?

"I don't want to be pitied," says M. from my group of fabulous friends, in one of our heart-to-hearts. Well of course, who wants to be pitied, except for some mother who insists on sitting alone in the dark.

I find a dictionary at home that defines the word 'pity' as feeling sorrow for the trouble and pain of others.

That said, I can understand why people don't want to be pitied. Because who shows pity? Whoever is higher in the food chain; God over man, adults over children, the healthy over the sick.

I look up the definition of 'empathy', and find; emotionally identifying with the thoughts or feelings of another person. Sympathy. Kindness.

So it seems that empathy occurs among equals, and one arouses in the other understanding and kindness. And what's wrong with that?

I don't give advice to people I don't know, especially since I personally can't stand those who bombard me with advice and words of wisdom. Yet, from my advanced age I can only suggest: Talk! Share!

You're the only ones who think that the people close to you or not so close, don't see that you're having trouble walking, or that you're trembling. You only think that your colleagues at work don't notice that you spilled your coffee again, and only *you* are certain that the people behind you on line at the supermarket can't tell that it's taking you hours to get your things on the conveyor, or to get your credit card out of your wallet.

Make it easier on your loved ones who see you trembling and faltering, to understand why.

No one has described the feeling of someone facing a loved one's pain better than the Israeli poet Lea Goldberg:

If you give me my share in your darkest fears,
I might have a little light.
If you unload on my shoulders the weight of your burden,
I might have a little relief,
and your pain shall be my gift, with loving hands I will carry it,
I will not tumble, I will not fall…

And what's wrong with someone close or a stranger, offering me assistance? If I need it, I'll be happy for the help and say thank you, and if I can handle it by myself – I'll smile and say thanks for offering, but no need. In any case we all say thank you (and please and I'm sorry) and that feels right to me. Because that way I enable **them,** too, to earn a good place in Heaven for themselves…

It's not pity - it's kindness. Understanding. Humanity at its best. Let them.

So if you, too, want to do a good deed, and join the party, every person who trembles, wobbles, doesn't recognize his or her own difficulties, and is diagnosed thanks to your openness and lack of shame in the disease – will help you, as well. Because if we're talking about good places at that table in the heavens, why shouldn't there be as many people there as possible? The more the merrier, and the more chance of having big blowout party, no expense spared.

Two years after being diagnosed, I think I can summarize my current situation.

Most mornings I wake up with a song in my heart and cheerfully prepare a healthy breakfast, and realize that if I once had worries and anxieties, today it's enough to wake up and know that I'm alive, feeling well, and a short inventory shows that today there is no pain, that I slept well, and I managed to put on my pants standing up (!!!) and without falling down. Good enough!

Some days I wake up to a beautiful day, and for a moment I feel like I'm the first person in the history of medicine that was cured of Parkinson's.

Is it because of the medication I take (no, dear Y., I will not list them now, because it's really irrelevant), or maybe thanks to the amount of physical exercise that I make sure to do according to the instructions of whoever has anything to do with the Parkinson's field? Or maybe it's the Mannitol? Or maybe really, like my professor says, it's a lot to do with my attitude toward the disease, my optimism and sense of humor? Or maybe it's everything together? Or maybe it really doesn't matter.

Not everything is rainbows and smiling happy people, like a Walt Disney movie. Not every day Sleeping Beauty wanders around the forest and sings, and all the forest animals, the birds, and squirrels, and Bambi and Thumper, gather round to listen.

First of all, Bambi and Thumper are from another movie, and second, I have my own issues; life with Parkinson's isn't a fairy tale.

Some nights I have unexplained pains that for no good reason travel from shoulder to back, knees to hips, and even if the pain is manageable and doesn't require that I take pain killers, even so it wakes me up from a good night's sleep.

After sleepless nights come days of stiffness and difficulty getting out of bed. On such mornings the usual song doesn't fill my heart, and the fear that I'm experiencing deterioration in my condition with no way back, makes me feel hurt and betrayed. I'm doing whatever is possible to delay the inevitable, so why is this happening to me?

Hurt and betrayed? That's the start of a bad mood, and that's definitely not the way to rise up and cheer. Ugh! (Who's to blame, anyway? Dammit, there's no one to fault...)

But I've even found a solution for the night pains. Guided meditation.

Years ago I went to a workshop, one of many, for self-development. Among other exercises we did guided meditation. The instructor told us to travel inside a carrot.

Everything at the top of the carrot was fresh, and green, and lovely, then orange and fresh and lovely, and boring and ridiculous. Ever since then I've had no tolerance for attempts to guide my imagination or wander around inside a carrot, eggplant, or potato.

Now, when I recalled my journey inside that carrot, I decided to use the technique in my own way. I started to mentally go through my body and let all my body parts know that they're about to feel good, and to let me sleep in peace. It's worked so far.

I continue to try and convince my brain, with the same technique, that I'm completely healthy and that it's creating an abundance of dopamine all by itself, and that I don't have Parkinson's. As soon as I succeed, I'll let you know.

I've noticed that when we meet with friends for coffee or dinner, everyone sits quiet and relaxed for a few hours, eating, talking, laughing, and I'm the only one rushing to the bathroom five or six times. The frequent runs when everyone else is sitting comfortably in the living room of our hosts, makes me uncomfortable. I think that I should suggest to our hosts, that just like we share gas expenses when we take a trip together, so I should offer to share the cost of municipal sewage.

At my advanced age, accompanied with my perhaps short experience with Parkinson's, but long experience in life, I already know that there are ups and downs, and whoever understands that knows that when you're on a downward wave, there will always be a wave that brings you back up.

And maybe I manage to remember that, because in difficult moments I always quote to myself the words of the wonderful English poet Percy Bysshe Shelley, who wrote, "If winter comes, can spring be far behind?"

Thanks for everything

Every time I visit a country I haven't been to yet, I make it a point to first learn the most important words – thank you.

Even the sternest and most irritable police officer at the Myanmar border melts like ice cream in the Asian heat, when a Western tourist smiles at him and says, *Yezuba*!

So here it is, in the languages I've picked up in my world travels:

Grazie mille Abigail Fleissig, and *Kussenem* Geula Altman, my good friends, who read my manuscript and laughed at the right places (BTW – does anyone know why it's still called a manuscript when it's been a computer file for a long time now?)

Merci, all the professionals who were happy to take on the task of writing the professional chapters of this book: Dr. Omer Porat, psychologist; Amir Carmin, chairman of the Israel Parkinson's Organization; Dan Vesely, entrepreneur; Galit Yogev, physiotherapist; Anat Greenberg, naturopathic practitioner; and Sinai Harel, qigong instructor.

And double extra *Muchas gracias* to Roni Peled,

who continues to dance with us twice a week, and *She-She* to Miri Gal who continues to make me move twice a week.

Kap kun ka to the artist Mike Leaf, our good friend, who was overjoyed at my idea and was quick to create all the illustrations in this book, with his typical sense of humor.

To my dear wonderful doctor Professor Nir Giladi, who jumped up from his chair when I told him about the book, went out to the waiting room and came back with his book, "Parkinson's Disease," and said, "Read the last chapter. It talks about dealing with the disease exactly the way you do, with a sense of humor and optimism. Edit it to fit your book and add it as an article by me." And so I did. *Danke viel mal...*

To my new friend, Raya Gonen; a meeting at one of Roni's groups and a duet from Carmen led to a great love story, *Toda* for her enormous help in promoting the book in the U.S.

My heartfelt *Thanks* go to Myra Hirschorn for providing me with all the info of the various foundations and organizations for PD in the u.s.a.

Spaciba to all the wonderful souls, complete strangers to me who cross my path for just a short moment, and reach out to help me when necessary.

And last but not least – *Muito obrigada* to my spouse, Amatzia, for everything he is.

PART II

What do the experts say?

ON ROSE-COLORED GLASSES, AND COPING WITH AN OPTIMISTIC VIEW

Prof. Nir Giladi

Director of Neurology Division, Ichilov Hospital, Tel- Aviv

Parkinson's is a serious disease that strikes the entire body, and affects the functioning and the life of the patient and the patient's family. Reading about it can certainly be distressful, in understanding how complex and multifaceted the disease is, how severe, and with no chance of complete recovery.

Nevertheless, I want to write this article from my personal point of view, after decades of treating thousands of families with Parkinson's, and accompanying patients from the diagnosis and along their path, to highlight the optimistic side of the journey.

The second half of life involves having to cope with various diseases, most of which have no cure, only optimal treatment. Modern medicine doesn't know how to cure hypertension, diabetes, heart disease or renal failure, retinal degeneration or arthritis.

Parkinson's is another one of those chronic diseases of

the second half of life, and fortunately there are many effective treatments.

In all the thousands of times I've had to inform a patient and family of a Parkinson's disease diagnosis, I've always made it clear that it is another one of the age-related diseases, and it should be treated as an uninvited escort. But since it has already entered your life, try to live with it in peace and acceptance, and not as an enemy. Alongside – not inside.

Patients and their partners who were able to develop a forgiving attitude, a calm acceptance in coping with the symptoms of the disease, learned that it's not as bad as it seems, and you can continue to live your life while being active, happy, and find personal growth. On the other hand, patients who fight a war against the disease and feel that their world had ended, suffer more from the disease, more damage to their quality of life, and usually require more medication and therefore face more frequent and difficult side effects.

We all want to maintain and improve our quality of life. The patient and partner's quality of life encompasses a wide range, and is very individual. Coping with Parkinson's requires physical and mental strength, adaptation and adjustment of expectations to reality. This process can be constructive and fulfilling. Many patients have told me how the need to cope with the disease and its many implications gave them new perspectives mid-life.

The insight as to what is important and what is more important, gave a new dimension to coping with the disease, and strange as it may sound, Parkinson's helped them to more correctly appreciate the good, as well as understanding where they are wasting energy. I know many couples that experienced an amazing improvement in their relationship as a result of the disease, renewed love and closeness, new significance, and a boost to intimacy that had waned over the years.

The actor Michael J. Fox, who was diagnosed with Parkinson's in his early 30s, described the positive process he underwent. He recently spoke of how the disease was a turning point for him, a source of growth and empowerment. He said that his quality of life vastly improved since the illness, on the personal level and the family level, and he founded a non-profit organization for the purpose of curing Parkinson's. Michael J. Fox has invested most of his efforts in recent years toward this end, and he says that this very meaningful activity has infused him with tremendous strength and a sense of satisfaction.

I also learned from my patients that optimism is the strongest and most effective medicine to deal with

Parkinson's disease. It improves all symptoms of the disease in both early and later stages. An optimistic attitude makes it easier to cope with the daily difficulties and the anxiety of what is to come.

I recommend to my patients that they see the world through rose-colored glasses.

An optimistic attitude and rose-colored glasses should also be adopted by the care-givers, thus also helping the patients and their families to cope. The medical team, and the primary caregiver who only see the negative and lacking, what's lost and will never be regained, broadcast a sense of hopelessness and helplessness to the patient and family. There is nothing more difficult for a patient than coping with such messages from a member of the medical team, and especially from the neurologist.

My work and accumulated experience over the years has only increased my level of optimism. We treat Parkinson's families better than ever. Science has made incredible breakthroughs in the past decade, and we don't see the change when we're partners in the process. But if I compare the knowledge and capabilities we had 15 years ago to what we have today, I have no doubt that we are on the way to cure Parkinson's.

It is clear to me that understanding the development process of the disease and the way it spreads in the body and brain opens the door to identifying the disease in its early stages and to stopping its development with a vaccine. I have long dreamed and believed that Parkinson's disease, within a decade or maybe a little longer, will be treated just like infectious diseases. We will vaccinate high-risk groups, and we will prevent progression of the disease in patients. We will do this while developing treatments that renew brain cells and clear them of the synuclein deposits that cause the degeneration.

Today, these treatment directions are already being evaluated in clinical research, and I believe that as a doctor I will be able to give this treatment to patients or to those at risk for the disease.

As an expression of our belief that we are on the way to beat the disease, at the Tel-Aviv Medical Center we invested our best efforts for the past ten years on a project for prevention of Parkinson's.

The bright future will come quicker only if families of patients join the efforts of science and medicine, and together will advance and spearhead the path to new discoveries and treatments for cure or prevention.

I will consider my path successful if the families of Parkinson's patients understand that it is a joint mission, if they wear those rose-colored glasses and join the fight to eradicate Parkinson's disease.

THE KEY TO LIFE WITH PARKINSON'S: EACH DAY IS A NEW CHALLENGE

Dr. Omer Porat, psychologist

Alexander the Great conquered his last kingdom 2,300 years ago. He asked his army officers, what's next? Their response, "we don't know of any lands that haven't been conquered yet." I will tell you Alexander's reply at the end.

Parkinson's disease is a challenge at every age, and it is undoubtedly a war against a worthy opponent, who usually does not lose. The only question is how it will win, - easily or with difficulty.

Many professionals and medical centers offer people struggling with the disease strategic counseling on how to defeat the disease, or at least to give it a fierce fight. Despite the advice and the many different kinds of medication, each day is a struggle. I've learned over the years in my professional career that sometimes, this war can actually be improved, and in some cases, made tolerable.

The key is in the basic understanding of how it operates and the games it plays between mind and body.

Parkinson's disease damages a specific part of the nervous system in a specific manner. If you're reading this, you must already know that this is mostly the dopaminergic system, which creates and releases the neurotransmitter dopamine. When the cells that create dopamine are active, they operate this nervous system, which affects our movement, thinking, motivation, and various emotions (especially enthusiasm and the desire to take action to achieve something).

We are beings who respond positively to positive events that we expect to happen. On the other hand, we are moody and sluggish if we perceive that we are facing a disappointment. If we have an in-depth understanding of this principle, we have the key to better coping with Parkinson's. Expectation for something positive or emotional raises the level of dopamine, which is released in the brain naturally, with no need for medication. Dopaminergic activity increases accordingly in the rest of the body, in various brain centers (for example cognitive), improving motor skill (movement), and also driving emotions, lifting from stagnation and apathy.

The function of system is to predict positive success. So the dopaminergic cell works harder when it thinks that something good is about to happen – but isn't one hundred percent sure (but wants to believe so). If it is certain that something good is going to happen – the cell doesn't act in a specific manner. If it is convinced that something bad will happen – it shuts down. That's the basis for understanding this system.

For example, if a man is stopped by a traffic cop, he is fearful. If the man happens to have Parkinson's, there's a good chance his trembling will intensify (and if he hasn't been diagnosed – he might start trembling for the first time). Why? Because the "dopaminergic faucet", those same dopamine-releasing cell clusters are temporarily repressed, which stops them from functioning.

Similarly, if a person is used to going to a concert every day, he will very quickly stop feeling any improvement from this activity. He's become used to it, and it no longer provides any special sense of enjoyment.

Alternately – and this is important for Parkinson's patients to understand – if every day we create an opportunity for a new positive experience, to get excited over something good or successful, to do something we've never experienced before, some new activity that is not familiar and not routine, we open the door for our body to do amazing things for us.

When Alexander the Great heard his officers say that there were no more lands to conquer, he sat and wept.

At least, that's what the history books say; apparently because he needed more and more conquests.

Parkinson's patients should learn something from him. Living with Parkinson's the right way, means conquering more peaks, fulfilling more wishes, realizing dreams and achieving goals, making life fascinating and exciting. That way, even as the disease progresses over the years – at least we know we gave it our best fight, that we are a worthy opponent.

TREATMENT WITH NUTRITION, HERBS, SUPPLEMENTS, AND MORE

Anat Greenberg – naturopathic practitioner

When a small region of the brain, called black matter, substantia nigra, starts to degenerate for some unknown reason, the nerve cells in the black matter are destroyed and the production of dopamine decreases. This creates an imbalance with acetylcholine, which becomes dominant and causes involuntary tremors at rest and when under stress, muscle rigidity, balance problems and instability when walking. Other symptoms may appear, such as loss of memory, speech difficulties, constipation, insomnia, anxiety, increased sweating, and more.

The disease develops slowly, and the decrease in quality of life is gradual. Nutritional therapy focuses on slowing the progress of the disease and easing the symptoms.

Nutrition should be natural, whole, and organic, with a high concentration of vitamins, minerals, antioxidants and Omega 3. Avoid processed or spoiled food, alcohol, and white sugar, which interfere with the proper functioning of the nervous system.

NATURAL NUTRITION

in the age of abundance we live in, it's very easy to buy prepared sauces, prepared salads, breakfast cereals, sweet and colorful dairy products, and other packaged foods in bottles, bags, plastic and carton, quick-mix powders that are not real foods and mostly comprised of sugar, salt, hydrogenated oils, food coloring and preservatives, artificial flavors, and other evils that are harmful not just for Parkinson's patients, but for everyone. Natural nutrition is home-cooked, made of ingredients as close to nature as possible, such as whole grains, legumes, fruits and vegetables, fresh and dried herbs, raw and unsalted nuts, almonds, and seeds, cold-pressed oils, healthy sweeteners such as natural date syrup, pure honey or maple syrup, Atlantic sea salt or Himalayan salt, which are natural salts rich in iodine and low sodium.

FRUITS AND VEGETABLES

These are the basics of a healthy kitchen. Buy fresh and seasonal in small quantities; best every 3-4 days and not once every two weeks. Frozen vegetables are an excellent alternative whenever you don't have fresh produce at home. Vegetables are essential. Fresh in salads, steamed, in soups, baked, stir-fried, as a side dish or the main dish. The more vegetables we eat, different types and the diversity of colors, the better we feel. Seasonal vegetables are cheaper and readily available, and usually are best for our bodies at the time. Orange, yellow, and dark green vegetables, fresh and cooked, are especially good for Parkinson's because they contain flavonoids. Recent studies show that flavonoids decrease the risk of developing Parkinson's disease.

GRAINS

Whole grains are best – whole grain rice, oats, rye, and spelt. Whole grains contain the entire grain kernel, vitamin-rich especially with B vitamins that are important for a healthy nervous system. Recently wheat has been connected to digestive problems and food allergies, and Parkinson's patients are advised to avoid wheat products, also whole wheat, couscous, burghul, pasta, breads, and wheat-based baked goods.

LEGUMES

Lentils of all colors, beans of all kinds, split peas, whole chickpeas, natural, frozen or sprouted. Choose legumes by their color. Old legumes don't look as good, and don't smell as good. Old legumes don't soften even after long cooking time. Buy from a reliable source with high turnover and closed packages. Research shows that white beans reduce the risk of developing Parkinson's disease.

HERBS

Buy in small quantities in reliable specialty stores, and if possible buy whole and grind at home.

OILS

Refined oils are not healthy. Cold-pressed oils are best; high-quality olive oil, and aromatic oils such as cold-pressed sesame and nut oils. Olive oil is best for seasoning and cooking, but don't let it get too hot, to the smoke point when it becomes oxidized and is harmful to your health. Cook with olive oil on low to medium heat and avoid burning the oil.

SWEETENERS

Limit your use of white sugar (and brown). Instead, use unrefined cane sugar, maple syrup, carob syrup, honey, and date syrup.

EGGS? CHICKEN? BEEF?

Studies suggest that limiting animal protein (eggs,

chicken, beef) significantly reduces Parkinson's symptoms. Legumes replace these proteins, together with whole grains or fish, especially North Sea fish such as salmon and tuna, halibut and hake. The protein is more easily digested, and they contain Omega 3, which is essential for the brain.

DAIRY

Studies show a direct link between high consumption of dairy products and quick progression of Parkinson's disease. It's better to avoid cow's milk and eat a little (if at all) natural full fat goat's milk yogurt.

ORGANIC

Organic food is grown without pesticides and without any artificial substances. The chemicals used in conventional agriculture to kill weeds and get rid of insects are harmful for Parkinson's patients. Organic food is highly recommended. If that isn't possible, wash fruits and vegetables thoroughly with ecological detergent, and cut off around 0.5 inch from each side. It's better to only buy organic herbs such as parsley, coriander, etc., because you can't get rid of pesticides.

OMEGA 3

Essential for healthy brain function, and have an anti-inflammatory effect on the body. Omega 3 is found in fish from the North Sea, as well as in ground flax seed and chia, and raw walnuts.

Food allergies can aggravate Parkinson's disease. A special elimination diet can identify allergenic foods and help to avoid them, to improve the condition of Parkinson's patients. This diet should be done under the supervision of a qualified naturopath.

Anti-oxidant medicinal herbs such as gingko biloba, ashwagandha, green tea, bacopa, and turmeric, fight free radicals that destroy cells and cause their degeneration. Other plants also protect the brain, such as rosemary, melissa, scutellaria, and sage. Sage and rosemary are known in herbal medicine as memory boosters and for enhancing cognitive capabilities. Recent studies prove that these are anti-oxidant herbs that protect brain cells and prevent degenerative diseases of the brain. Melissa, black horehound, and scutellaria are calming herbs, anti-depressants that increase the activity of the neurotransmitter GABA, and help to sleep.

Supplements recommended for treating Parkinson's are also anti-oxidants: alpha lipoic acid, Vitamin E, Vitamin C, co-enzyme Q10, quercetin, grape seed extract, and berries. Supplements should be used under the supervision of a qualified naturopath.

Reflexology is highly recommended to balance the body, for relaxation, for circulation, and to strengthen the central nervous system.

Aromatherapy – lavender, rose, and geranium oil are very helpful for stress relief. Use in the bath, as massage oil, and in an oil diffuser.

Bach flowers – Rescue Remedy helps to relax. Honeysuckle helps let go of the past, focus on the present, and look forward to the future. Oak essence helps to gather strength and fight the disease. A certified Bach practitioner can help find a formula of essences to help each patient.

PHYSIOTHERAPY FOR PARKINSON'S

Dr. Galit Yogev-Seligman, physiotherapist and lecturer

Physiotherapy for Parkinson's enables maximal quality of movement, functional independence, increases overall physical fitness, and minimizes secondary complications. In addition, the physiotherapist helps and instructs the patient in self-care and safety, fits walking and mobility aids, and advises on how to adapt the home and environment.

Physiotherapy treatments address a number of relevant aspects of a Parkinson's patient.

1. General physical ability - muscle strength, flexibility, cardio, coordination and balance are essential for daily activities that are affected by Parkinson's disease. Physiotherapy treatments emphasize teaching and practicing specific exercises to maintain physical capabilities, while addressing specific impairments of the disease. Intensive daily physical exercise focused on the relevant problems of the patient can relieve symptoms (rigidity, weakness and fatigue, lack of balance), slow the progression of the disease, and has a positive effect on the brain.

2. Transitions – as the disease progresses, many patients find it difficult to perform transitions on their own (such as movement in bed, transition from lying down to sitting, from sitting in a chair to standing, and more), The physiotherapist instructs and practices diverse techniques and strategies with the patient, to make these transitions easier.

3. Balance – the problem of balance in Parkinson's stems from a combination of factors. The job of the physiotherapist is to identify the main factors for the balance disorder, outline a treatment plan, and instruct the patient and family how to reduce the risk of falls.

4. Walking – problems for Parkinson's patients include slow walking, dragging feet, freezing episodes, or transition to quick walk/involuntary run (festination). As part of the treatment for walking disorders, the physiotherapist will instruct the patient on compensation strategies – simple techniques using various types of sensory stimuli (in professional literature called external cues), which lead to improved mobility and walking. These techniques activate healthy parts of the brain, circumventing the part of the brain damaged by Parkinson's, thus enabling better movement. Another compensation strategy –

cognitive, improves mobility through concentrating on specific aspects, for example the length of stride or swinging the arms. These techniques have been scientifically proven effective in improving walking and other functions such as getting up and mobility in bed.

5. Upper extremity function – practicing gross and fine motor skills of the upper extremities, including compensation techniques, for example writing.

6. Instructing family/chaperone and fitting aids – the physiotherapist instructs the family/chaperone/caregiver how to help the patient. Instruction includes performing safe and effective transitions, demonstrating how to perform exercises independently, accompaniment while walking, and encouraging activity to the extent possible, while guarding the patient's safety, as well as how to prevent bedsores in bedridden patients or patients in wheelchairs in advanced stages of the disease. The physiotherapist will suggest modifications in the home and physical environment to improve daily functioning and reduce risk of falls. In addition, fitting mobility and walking aids such as walkers, wheelchair, and instructions on proper use of these aids.

7. Physiotherapy includes, as needed, techniques to mitigate and cope with pain and breathing exercises.

8. In summary, physiotherapy for Parkinson's patients is customized for each patient according to functional needs and capabilities and includes:

- Weekly training/exercise program to maintain physical capabilities
- Practice and instruction in performing transitions
- Practice and instruction for compensation techniques to mitigate walking disorders
- Practice and instruction to address balance issues and to prevent falls
- Instruction on modifications to home and environment.

ON THE ADVANTAGES OF MOVEMENT

Miri Gal, certified Feldenkrais instructor

The Feldenkrais Method is the story of Moshe Feldenkrais' personal journey toward understanding the depths of the mind and body, while trying to heal himself from a serious knee injury to avoid surgery.

Feldenkrais (1904 – 1984); Jewish, Israeli, a scientist with a doctorate in physics and degree in electrical engineering, and a black belt in judo, developed his method in the 1940s and 50s. He studied the principles of Eastern martial arts, the intricacies of the human body, studied infant development, practiced guided meditation techniques, hypnosis, and autosuggestion. He noticed that animals are born with movement capabilities, and can immediately move about freely. In contrast, humans go through a long learning process.

A baby is born with great potential for mobility, but cannot crawl, turn over, sit, and walk. In the first few months of life, babies teach themselves spatial awareness. There is no structured program; learning is spontaneous, through trial and error. Thus movement patterns are created in the nervous system, embedded and/or stored in the brain, and used as the baby matures.

The advantage of movement according to patterns is that it enables us to move automatically, without having to think before each move. It becomes a problem when it the patterns no longer suit us.

Feldenkrais realized that the severe pain he suffered from did not stem from the physical injury to his knee, but rather from movement habits that were no longer appropriate for him that he acquired after the injury. He came to the conclusion that to heal himself, he had to learn to move in a way that suited him better. He successfully changed the way he stood and walked, which enabled his knee to return to its normal functioning. In the same manner he helped many others, among them David Ben-Gurion, Moshe Dayan, and the violinist Yehudi Menuchin.

The method, developed in Tel Aviv, is taught around the world, and recommended by orthopedists, psychologists, neurologists, neurosurgeons, and others.

Why do habits we acquired no longer suit us?

The nervous system is responsible for the muscles, and thus controls our body's ability to move.

When the body is fit, the efforts are distributed harmoniously between the muscles, skeleton, and connective tissues. Over the years we gradually reduce the range of movement we acquired as infants, and movements that aren't used are forgotten. In addition, we acquire new movement habits that come from injuries we've sustained, and short-cuts that we make, such as using our hands or feet instead of moving the entire body.

Because these movement habits do not suit us, they disrupt the balance of movement in our bodies. Movement becomes cumbersome and painful.

The mind-body connection is at the basis of the Feldenkrais Method – the physical condition of our body is directly affected by stress, or ugly memories. They activate the nervous system and cause a muscular reaction. If the reaction repeats itself it becomes a pattern that damages the body's movement abilities. Practicing the method improves physical capabilities, and with that the emotional state.

IS IT POSSIBLE TO LEARN AND ACQUIRE NEW MOVEMENT HABITS?

In the past, it was believed that the brain cannot change. The brain was considered a machine, and the moment part of it was damaged, there was no replacement. Today we know that the brain is flexible and everyone can re-program the way his or her brain works.

In effect, we only use a small part of our brain, so if a certain section is damaged, the parts that are not in use can undergo a process of change and replace the damaged area.

Feldenkrais realized that movement patterns are wired into the nervous system, and new wiring can be achieved that will suit us better. As soon as a new pattern is appropriate it is used, and the old pattern is forgotten. He discovered that performing certain movements, or even imagining them, can create new connections in the nervous system, thus changing the structure of the brain and the way it functions.

HOW DOES THE METHOD WORK?

The foundation of the system is creating awareness of our body and the way we move. Observation and awareness enable us to move in a way that is appropriate for us.

We are used to making efforts to succeed, to be highly motivated. However, willpower doesn't' help to develop awareness. Neither does over exertion, which increases muscle tension.

Classes are taught in a group and the instructor gives verbal instructions on how to perform the movements. Most of the exercises are performed lying on a mat on the floor, which cancels the need to deal with gravity and thus enables the muscles, whose work is essential while standing, to relax.

The movements are small and easy, repeated many times slowly, while searching for continuity of motion that is best for each person. Thus excess muscle tension is reduced and enables more correct movement.

The nervous system learns beneficial movements, and creates a long-term change in movement habits. Practice makes the body more flexible, and enables effortless, free, harmonious, and stable movement.

In individual lessons (FI), the student lies on a treatment bed and the instructor moves the student rather than giving verbal instructions. The instructor's touch and manipulations enable better function for the student and enables the nervous system to find a new and more appropriate path for movement.

FELDENKRAIS AND PARKINSON'S

The Feldenkrais Method is one of the most recommended techniques for coping with Parkinson's disease. The slow movements calm the nervous system, relax muscle tension, improve posture, balance, and coordination, and enable learning new ways of movement.

A study conducted at the Federal University of Brazil found that the Feldenkrais Method improves the mood of Parkinson's patients, and their quality of life. The method enables easier movement, flexibility, and balance in Parkinson's patients, and therefore better control over the entire body.

ON THE WONDERS OF DANCE

Roni Peled, movement therapist, B.A. behavioral
Sciences, M.A. Dance Therapy

A study in 2017 based on MRI found that dancing results in neuroplasticity. Many other studies show improvement in motoric, cognitive, and emotional indices among people coping with Parkinson's who incorporate dance into their lives.

Recently, dance has become a mainstream treatment for Parkinson's patients, but I came into the field by chance, right before the big change.

I always knew that I wanted to channel my professional career toward emotional therapy. I chose to study psychology for my undergraduate degree and meanwhile, as a student, I trained to be a ballroom dance instructor.

I taught individuals and groups. During my studies, I felt that I kept meeting psychology on the dance floor. I realized that movement serves the dancers far beyond their initial purpose – to learn to dance. I felt how each person dived into in-depth and individual work. I found that beyond the dance, every person who came to the dance floor was looking for something different, something lacking – body image, initiative, communication, daring, commitment, listening, femiminity/masculinity, leadership, freedom, control…an endless list!

This realization was fascinating for me, so I looked for a professional track that would provide me with the tools for observation, understanding, and accompaniment of people's struggles, incorporating the mind and the body as inseparable elements. That is how I got to movement therapy

I studied at Lesley University for my M.A. with a focus on Dance Movement Therapy. I did my internship at a Maccabi Healthcare Services mental health clinic, where I treated people suffering from depression and anxiety, mostly resulting from physical illness and traumas. I learned how emotions react directly to physical decline and vice versa, how with the help of the body it's possible to build and return confidence, vitality, and love of life.

During my internship I met Rafi Eldor, at the studio where I taught dance. He entered the studio an introverted and withdrawn man. We started with an English waltz. During the class, Rafi told me about the Parkinson's and his feeling that dance could help him cope with the disease. He came in every day for private lessons, joined groups, and practiced and prepared for every class,

At a certain stage, I felt as if dance for him had

turned from a coping tool for Parkinson's to a way of life, a passion. He didn't just come to improve motor functions and stability, and also not to learn another rhumba step; he came to connect with himself, his body, soul, and to life.

Today, Rafi Eldor is a name recognized by every Parkinson's patient in Israel. Eldor is a Professor of Economics with expertise in risk management, and an impressive international professional record in these fields. After he was diagnosed with Parkinson's he started doing preventive physical activity and especially dance. He performs with professional dancers, and a video clip of him dancing with Ana Aronov won first prize at an international conference on Parkinson's in the United States.

In my profession, movement therapy, you learn to observe the body, to investigate, understand, see what's lacking, what is in excess. I started learning movement habits and movement disorders that repeated themselves. I found myself slowly developing a work method adapted to the unique symptoms of Parkinson's, into which I incorporate the world of ballroom dancing.

Of course, Parkinson's is different in each individual, but between the dances, the rhythms, and the diverse possibilities of movement, it's possible to find a solution for many motor function issues and limitations. The treatment can be suited to movement classes for the emotional and physical needs of people who come to cope with and manage their individual conditions. I later came to realize that the common element is the wondrous effect of the music; an external trigger that grants rhythm to individual movement and connects the group. I also realized that dance is an intuitive, natural, and enjoyable means to approach most of the limitations of the disease, through indirect rather than direct channels.

I came to the realization that this tool, the dance, is strong and significant in coping with Parkinson's and that I should try to share this insight, expose it and be exposed within the community. The first step was to start working with a group of Parkinson's patients, where for the first time I implemented what was becoming my treatment method.

The Israel Parkinson's Organization invited me to start a group in Tel Aviv, and then in Petach Tikva. As I became established as a movement and dance therapist for people with Parkinson's, I was invited to share my method with a number of medical facilities, to present the therapeutic options. In lectures and discussions that I had with professionals in the various units for movement disorders, I shared my experience and belief that movement and dance can be an amazing complement to a Parkinson's treatment program.

The feedback was ambivalent. Although clearly it was correct physical activity adapted to Parkinson's, but there were also some reservations, as there is some element of risk in movement and dance. Furthermore, the field has spiritual and abstract connotations, especially in light of my philosophy, which talks about the fact that the mental state is the basis for coping with the physical aspect of the disease. Nevertheless, Ichilov Hospital showed interest and offered me to establish a group within the framework of the movement disorder unit, where to this day I teach, together with a speech therapist. The group has been in existence now for more than three years, and is being researched by the unit.

The study shows improvement in voice, motor capabilities, and quality of life among people with Parkinson's participating in the group.

For the most part, coping with Parkinson's, a multisystem disease, is characterized by drug treatments, supplements, experimenting with various types of physical activities (mostly unfamiliar to the person's body), strenuous physical therapy, and alternative medicine. The body may instantly become a functional tool, damaged and requiring fixing, improving, and changing.

That's the very moment when it's important to stop, reorganize, and try to stop that trend, which in many cases brings to alienation and antagonism toward the body. The unique tool of movement and dance offers a way for Parkinson's patients to work with their bodies, to maximize their physical capabilities and return the belief in themselves and the trust in their bodies.

Many people ask me if my occupation is difficult, or sad. And I always say, on the contrary, there are very few occupations that enable you to influence, to touch, and see improvement. I give all of myself to my patients every day anew, and get back double the energy, optimism, and appreciation.

MIND-BODY MEDICINE, QIGONG

Sinai Harel, Chinese Medicine practitioner

Head of qigong teacher training at Wingate Institute

Qigong is the energetic branch of Chinese medicine, integrating work on the mind and body. The purpose is to train and introduce the student to the world of "movement therapy."

This is a powerful therapy tool, essentially movement exercises that engage the healing powers of the body to our benefit. It means: cultivation of energy (qi in Chinese) and can also be called the art of relaxation, or meditation in movement. The Western world was exposed to qigong only 25 years ago, and before that it was a well-kept secret for hundreds of years as a "national treasure," the best kept in China.

Contrary to other Chinese healing tools, qigong is unique in the demand for personal involvement of every practitioner; it can also be called "self-acupuncture." Qigong practice prevents a wide range of medical problems; the first and most important result is improving vitality. This is built through practice: changing breathing patterns, working on posture, flexibility, self-control and concentration.

Daily practice of qigong sharpens awareness of

the body. Our body needs and is thirsty for daily communication with our mind, saying, "You need my health and I need your attention." This contract is made every day between two entities. This brave partnership is not to be taken for granted. Therapeutic movement is important and necessary for our health. When this condition exists – other systems activate to heal and renew our bodies more energetically.

Qigong practice is accompanied by in-depth work on activating, changing, and the flow of qi, which enables not only health, but also enjoyment of our body. Diligent practice will bring significant development and change in the practitioner's life style, and significant improvement in every aspect of health: joyfulness, relaxation, concentration, coordination, posture, spatial awareness and flexibility of thought. The Chinese views anything that flows and is not stuck, as healthy. The image is of smooth door hinges that move freely and therefore don't get rusty.

THE LANGUAGE OF QIGONG IS THE MERIDIANS

Qigong works according to the unique discovery of Chinese medicine: the meridians are a 3,000 –year-old Chinese discovery, perhaps the greatest discovery in the field of Chinese medicine. The Chinese discovered the code of the meridians (energy lines that connect the mind and body), after in-depth observation of the

212 | ALONA GOLAN SADAN

body, the feelings and senses. Qigong as a therapy tool is especially powerful – every movement in our body activates a meridian that expresses an emotional aspect. Since the mind is not physical and the body is felt through the senses, treating the mind is implemented through the body. In fact, moving a bodily organ drives a meridian that represents an emotional aspect.

The direction and pace determined in advance enables proper and balanced flow of energy in the meridian. A meridian represents correlation between a person's body, feelings, emotions, connection to society and to nature. For example:

Pelvic motion to the right and left develops stability, which is very important for Parkinson's patients, improves hearing, balances qi in the kidneys, releases fears - and correlates with the water element in nature.

Forward and backward movement of the spine develops flexibility, improves vision, balances qi in the liver and releases anger – and correlates with the wood element in nature.

Up and down movement in the chest develops alertness, improves sense of smell, balances qi in the lungs, releases sadness – and correlates with the metal element in nature.

Movement that extends the neck develops coordination, improves sense of touch, balances qi of the heart, releases passion – and correlates with the element of fire in nature.

Movement concentrated in the stomach region develops concentration, improves sense of taste, balances qi in the spleen, releases worries, and correlates with the earth element in nature.

A tangible example of this order compares the harmonious function of government hierarchy, with each minister in charge of his field with respect to the entire system. For example: the ruler, the Caesar is the heart, Minister of Defense is in charge of the liver, Foreign Minister – health, Minister of the Interior – spleen, and Minister of the Treasury – kidneys.

Treating the five main systems in our body will also treat their respective emotional balance: reproductive system – fears, nervous system – anger, circulatory system - agitation, digestive system – worry, and respiratory system – sadness. Observing this process is called meditation. In itself, it is not enough. Incorporating physical practice called "meditation in movement" – is qigong.

What is the difference is between qigong and tai chi? Tai chi is a recognized and popular form of qigong. Specifically, it is a style of qigong that develops the use of qi for offense or defense. It is the martial form of qigong, and part of the soft Chinese martial arts.

Daily qigong practice is very effective for self-treatment, without the help of a therapist.

These diverse movements work in special codes that connect between man and nature. This attention to our body enables healthy nature to lead the body, rather than behavioral patterns that feed from one culture or another. These movements were carefully accumulated over thousands of years, and today can be seen in tens of thousands of parks in China, and have gained worldwide recognition.

Qigong advocates accepting personal responsibility to strengthen and balance the body. Patients treat themselves, contrary to the passivity of acupuncture or touch therapy. The powerful effect of qigong practice on the mind and body is immeasurable.

As a therapy, qigong, which is a movement practice, is a methodical medical tool. As such, it has to meet the stringent requirements of the rules of Chinese Medicine: yin-yang, the five elements, and the meridians.

I acquired this insight during the time I lived in Japan and studied the sources of qigong. To this day, over more than 30 years, I bring everything that I have learned every day, to my work.

ON MANNITOL RESEARCH AND CLINICROWD

Danny Vesely – entrepreneur

When other people around me were investing in the stock market, I invested in friends. And…the yield was more than tenfold.

The fact that I was very active and athletic increased the intensity of the shock from my circle of friends, when they heard the diagnosis - Parkinson's at the age of 55!

All I could do was research a way to find a cure. Everyone got onboard as if it was a decree from on high, and all in the name of friendship.

Eran, a friend of mine, found himself at 40,000 feet sitting next to Professor Danny Segal, both of them on their way to a medical conference in Hong Kong. Eran learned that his companion was the head of a significant trial at the Tel Aviv University neurology laboratory, to find a substance that may help Parkinson's patients. For Eran, this was enough to connect between me and the professor, for continued investigation, analysis, and a verdict.

I learned the following:

The cause of the disease is the protein alpha

synuclein, which apparently develops in the intestines, climbs to a certain point in the brain, and from this vantage point attacks the dopamine cells, which are directly responsible for our motor functions.

After screening various substances, the professors Segal, Gazit, and Masliah determined that the most worthy for comprehensive, in-depth research is Mannitol – an FDA and EU-approved sweetener for diabetics. Mannitol is found in some vegetables, and some say its name stems from the manna bread that the Israelites ate in the desert.

In 2013, the three professors published a paper in a renowned medical journal on the remarkable and surprising results of their research. Fruit flies and lab mice were observed with an up to 70% reduction of the aggressive protein that causes Parkinson's, and a return of most of their motor function.

Alongside the cheers of celebration, on the path to a cure for the disease that affects 30,000 people in Israel and around 10 million people around the world, what's left is to complete the process and be convinced that others will respond in a similar manner.

The common path of transition from just another substance – to a drug approved by the regulator, the FDA, must pass through the following stations: the willingness of a hospital or pharma company laboratory to set out on the journey, raise between three to five million dollars, approval of the Helsinki Commission, recruit a few dozen patients who are willing to take part in trials, and a few who are willing to be a control group. And even then, any findings will take at least five years.

In a meeting with Professor Segal, and with two friends in the startup world, we realized the essence of the problem, analyzing the element that stood in our way: from the findings of the trial to an approved medication.

Mannitol is an existing substance, readily available to anyone. Therefore, it isn't possible to register a patent on it, and there is no business model that will yield an appropriate financial return. In the absence of an investor, the substance remained useless on the laboratory shelves, joining thousands of other substances, medications for other diseases, on the shelf.

From the status of searching for a cure for Parkinson's we turned to thinking about other diseases that are neglected solely because there is no financial gain.

With the help of two other friends, from the fields of pharma and computers, we established an initiative called CliniCrowd, which leans on and is nurtured by the experiences of the wisdom of the crowd, and provides the crowd with educated insights.

The essence of the initiative is to create a kind of alternative to the standard track of drug approval; to confirm or facilitate efficacy of a substance approved for human consumption to help or relieve a certain disease, through reporting by the crowd.

We work via an Internet platform: www.clinicrowd. info; to drive patients to choose to experiment, to take the substance and periodically report their medical status, toward gaining insights and drawing conclusions.

Participants fill out a questionnaire with personal details, disease status, medications they take, supplements, activities, etc. Gathering massive amounts of data enables trend analysis and to extract recommendations based on the reports of the "overwhelming majority."

We believe in the existence of effective and safe substances – there are many substances that do not get the attention they deserve from investors in drug development even though they may relieve, decrease, prevent, or cure diseases/symptoms, at a reasonable cost. We believe in changing the nature of the current interface between patient and doctor – availability and accessibility of information to patients in the face of limited attention and inhumane schedules that don't leave doctors the time to be updated on available innovations.

The abovementioned leads to a new situation, in

which in most cases the patient will know more about the disease than the doctor. From here, the next step is to shift disease management – to the patient.

CliniCrowd makes testimonials and data from thousands of other patients available to patients, and helps provide confidence and support in the process of risk management and decision-making in managing the disease. When a patient is exposed to the reports of hundreds of people in the same situation on the outcome of taking a substance, and the fact that it caused no harm, it raises confidence in the decision.

We believe in the importance and power of the community – CliniCrowd encourages the creation of communities (for each disease) that have the power to serve as support groups (internally) and as influence groups (externally).

CliniCrowd is a social platform for managing the database of questionnaires for substances approved as safe for human consumption by the FDA, but with no economic incentive for official clinical trials even though they have the potential to help patients. We launched a secure platform that investigates and validates solutions for diseases that have been researched scientifically, are safe, inexpensive, and available, which have not yet been tested because of lack of financial incentive. These solutions can lead to a healthy and better life for people with various diseases and medical conditions, including Parkinson's, Alzheimer's, and others. The platform provides analysis and insights attained through the wisdom of the crowd and enables participants and the crowd to better manage their personal symptoms and improve and influence the lives of all of us. CliniCrowd is not a pharma company and does not provide medical advice. Rather, it provides data and connects the dots for a comprehensive picture derived from many reports, and which uses the law of large numbers.

MANNITOL AND PARKINSON'S DISEASE – PROOF OF CONCEPT AND LEVERAGING THE EXPERIENCES OF THE CROWD – PRELIMINARY RESULTS LOOK PROMISING

Since the launch of the platform in 2017, approximately 1500 Parkinson's patients from 42 countries around the world decided to test Mannitol through the CliniCrowd platform. Of them, 78 who took Mannitol for more than six months (the placebo effect on Parkinson's can last for six months) report through the CliniCrowd platform:

56% reported an improvement in Parkinson's disease and their symptoms (despite the deteriorating nature of the disease)

90% got their sense of smell back

86% improved facial expressions

81% improvement in walking

80% decrease in hallucinations

78% improvement in energy and vitality

77% decrease in muscle spasms

For more details, on these and other indications, you can join our crowd-based surveys at clinicrowd.info

A few important notes:

CliniCrowd does not provide medical advice

It is not a clinical trial; it is an investigation based on reports of patients who chose to report the status of their disease while taking Mannitol in addition to the other medications prescribed by their doctors.

CliniCrowd does not sell Mannitol and does not cooperate with any manufacturer of distributor of Mannitol.

The results are based only on patients who decided to take Mannitol and report to the community.

Conclusive proof is still far off. It requires perseverance, patience, and especially participation of as many patients as possible! The more patients join the more power to create the necessary change and examine substances that can help cure diseases despite the lack of financial gain.

ON U.S GOVERNMENT BENEFITS AND INSURANCE

The U.S. government provides benefits and care coverage to those in need.

On this page we outline some programs that may help people living with Parkinson's disease. Remember to keep any potentially relevant paperwork you receive from an employer, an insurer, a government agency or an advocate on your behalf and to keep copies of everything that you submit.

SOCIAL SECURITY

In addition to traditional retirement benefits, the Social Security Administration (SSA) also provides benefits to qualifying individuals with disabilities. Visit the Benefit Eligibility Screening Tool (BEST) and the Disability Planner to see if you or a loved one qualify for SSA disability programs.

SOCIAL SECURITY DISABILITY INSURANCE (SSDI)

If you live with Parkinson's disease, are below 65 years of age and are unable to work due to your Parkinson's disease and/or other condition, you might be entitled to SSDI benefits. These are income supplements for people whose employment is limited due to a disability. Read more about SSDI or call 1-800-772-1213 to learn more.

It can take a few months for SSDI to kick in. During that period, applicants may be eligible for Supplemental Security Income (SSI) benefits from the government.

SSDI beneficiaries are automatically eligible for Medicare after collecting SSDI benefits for 24 months. They may also be eligible for Medicaid but must submit a separate Medicaid application. See below for more information on those programs. For further information, read the Social Security guide to Medicare.

SUPPLEMENTAL SECURITY INCOME (SSI)

SSI provides a monthly cash stipend to people with disabilities who need help meeting their basic needs for shelter, food and clothing. It differs from SSDI in that it is based on financial need only. Read more about SSI or call 1-800-772-1213 to learn more.

People diagnosed with multiple system atrophy, a type of parkinsonism, may qualify for a fast-tracked application under the compassionate allowances condition initiative, which is reserved for applicants whose medical conditions almost always meet Social Security's disability standards.

REVISED RULES FOR DETERMINING ELIGIBILITY

Beginning September 29, 2016, the Social Security Administration (SSA) will be using new criteria to evaluate Parkinson's disease for disability insurance. This marks the first time the SSA has incorporated the non-motor aspects of Parkinson's disease, such as cognitive functioning, into its criteria for evaluating SSDI applications.

View comments from the SSA about the new rules and read MJFF's blog on the topic.

MEDICARE

Medicare provides health care services for people 65 and older and people younger than age 65 with disabilities. There are several components to Medicare:

Part A covers inpatient hospital stays, skilled nursing facility stays, home health visits (also covered under Part B) and hospice care

Part B covers physician visits, outpatient services, preventive services and home health visits

Part C refers to the Medicare Advantage program, through which beneficiaries can enroll in a private health plan and receive all Medicare-covered benefits

Part D covers both brand-name and generic pre-scription drugs; this coverage is provided through third-party companies known as prescription drug plans (PDP)

Medicare supplement (Medigap) is insurance sold by private companies that can help pay for some health care costs that Medicare does not cover

Each state has a State Health Insurance Assistance Program to help Medicare beneficiaries find the most appropriate insurance options.

MEDICARE THERAPY CAPS

The Balanced Budget Act of 1997 created limits, or caps, on the amount of outpatient physical, occupational and speech-language therapy a Medicare beneficiary can receive each calendar year. There is currently a combined $2,010 yearly cap for physical therapy and speech-language therapy, and a separate $2,010 yearly cap for occupational therapy. Once those amounts are reached, beneficiaries who require additional services in the calendar year are responsible for 100 percent of the cost. In addition to the caps, a manual medical review is required once a beneficiary hits $3,700 in therapy services.

To mitigate the impact of these caps, Congress created an exceptions process for services deemed medically necessary. However, the exceptions process was temporary and expired on December 31, 2017. The Parkinson's community has long advocated for a complete repeal of the caps to ensure people with Parkinson's have access to medically necessary therapy services. Until this is achieved, the Foundation and other patient advocacy groups will push for Congress to reinstate the exceptions process.

MEDICARE IMPROVEMENT STANDARD

Up until 2013, the "improvement standard" was an inaccurate policy being arbitrarily applied by Medicare providers, contractors and adjudicators that required beneficiaries to show improvement to continue receiving physical, occupational and speech-language therapy. For people with chronic degenerative conditions like Parkinson's, therapy is not intended to result in improvement; it's used to help maintain function and increase quality of life. Therefore, people with PD could be denied therapy services under this inaccurate "improvement standard".

The "improvement standard" was challenged by several patients and advocacy groups, including the former Parkinson's Action Network, in the case of Jimmo v. Sebelius. The parties reached a settlement in January 2013 declaring Medicare beneficiaries cannot be denied coverage for physical, occupational and speech-language therapy, as well as other select services (including skilled nursing facilities, inpatient rehabilitation facilities and home health), solely for lack of improvement. The Centers for Medicare and Medicaid Services (CMS), which administers the Medicare program, was given one year to update its policy manual and execute a nationwide education campaign for all who make Medicare determinations.

Unfortunately, while the policy manual has been updated, confusion remains and people are still being denied coverage. In Spring 2016, the parties returned to court to pursue further legal action to ensure the Jimmo settlement is fully and accurately implemented.

In February 2017, the court ordered CMS to execute a "corrective action plan" to ensure beneficiaries are no longer being denied coverage due to the "improvement standard." The plan includes:

- A new CMS webpage dedicated to Jimmo
- A published corrective statement disavowing the improvement standard
- A posting of frequently asked questions
- New training for contractors making coverage decisions

- The corrective action plan must be complete and implemented by September 4, 2017.

MEDICAID

Medicaid is a joint federal-state program that provides health care services primarily to low-income individuals. Among those potentially eligible for coverage are people with disabilities and those who receive federally assisted income maintenance payments, such as Supplemental Security Income (read more on that program above). Because state governments contribute a substantial amount of funds to Medicaid, benefits vary widely around the country. Nearly all programs help pay for prescription drugs.

For more information, visit the Medicaid website or find contact information for the Medicaid office in your area.

CONSOLIDATED OMNIBUS BUDGET RECONCILIATION ACT (COBRA)

The Consolidated Omnibus Budget Reconciliation Act (COBRA) stipulates that when an employee loses health care coverage under an employer-sponsored plan, he or she can elect to continue coverage under that plan for a set period of time on a self-pay basis. COBRA applies most frequently in instances when an employee is laid off (for reasons other than "gross misconduct") or his or her hours are reduced. The law also applies to the employee's dependents in the event of divorce, the employee's death or other situations.

Generally, employers are required to offer access to their health care plan for 18 months after the employee is terminated or his or her hours are reduced. That period is extended to 29 months for an individual who is determined to be disabled under the Social Security Administration guidelines.

VETERANS AND PARKINSON'S

In 2001, the Department of Veterans Affairs (VA) created six specialized centers known as the Parkinson's Disease Research, Education and Clinical Centers (PADRECCs). These centers serve veterans affected by Parkinson's disease through state-of-the-art clinical care, education and research. Each PADRECC services a large geographic area and is staffed by movement disorder specialists, neurosurgeons and other Parkinson's disease experts who assist veterans in managing their disease.

In order to serve veterans diagnosed with Parkinson's disease nationwide, the PADRECCs created the Consortium Centers, which offer specialized Parkinson's disease and movement disorder specialty care to veterans who cannot travel to a PADRECC. Currently, 51 Consortium Centers work collaboratively with the

PADRECCs to ensure the highest level of care for all veterans.

Locate a PADRECC or Consortium Center.

TRAUMATIC BRAIN INJURY

In December 2013, the VA finalized a regulation that makes it easier for some veterans with moderate or severe traumatic brain injury (TBI) who also have parkinsonism, including Parkinson's disease, to receive additional disability pay. This regulation impacts veterans living with TBI who also have Parkinson's disease, certain types of dementia, depression, unprovoked seizures or certain diseases of the hypothalamus and pituitary glands. If a veteran had a moderate or severe TBI as a result of service and also has Parkinson's, then the Parkinson's will also be considered service connected for the calculation of VA disability compensation.

AGENT ORANGE

In 2010, the VA recognized Parkinson's disease as associated with exposure to Agent Orange or other herbicides during military service in Vietnam. Veterans who develop Parkinson's disease and were exposed to Agent Orange or other herbicides during military service do not have to prove a connection between their disease and military service to be eligible to receive VA disability compensation. Veterans diagnosed with Parkinson's disease who served in-country or on the inland waterways of Vietnam between January 9, 1962, and May 7, 1975, are presumed exposed to Agent Orange or other herbicides.

This decision was based on an Institute of Medicine report, "Veterans and Agent Orange: Update 2008," which stated there was "suggestive but limited evidence that exposure to Agent Orange and other herbicides used during the Vietnam War is associated with an increased chance of developing Parkinson's disease".

Learn more about the VA's position on Parkinson's disease and Agent Orange.

CARE PARTNERS

The VA offers a number of support services for loved ones who care for a veteran through the VA Caregiver Program. You can locate a local Caregiver Support Coordinator or call the Caregiver Support Line at 1-855-260-3274

OTHER DISABILITY POLICIES

Many employers offer short-term and/or long-term disability plans that employees can choose to put money into while they are working. After leaving work because of a disability, qualified employees receive a portion of their salary while they are disabled. Private-sector plans usually begin paying out within a period of months after a disability begins. That compares favorably with most government disability programs, which can take a year or more to approve a disability claim and begin disbursing payment. Some private plans pay a set amount regardless of what an insured patient receives from Social Security, while other plans may offset the benefits they pay by whatever disability payments the insured may receive from Social Security.

CONGRESSIONAL ASSISTANCE

Members of Congress can provide assistance to constituents who are applying for government benefits. Your senators or representative may be able to help with:

- Tracking a misdirected benefits payment
- Filling out a government form
- Applying for Social Security, veterans', education and other federal benefits
- In some cases, your senators or representative may be able to help expedite a Social Security disability claim. Your elected official can open a congressional inquiry into the status of your claim and it may result in your application being processed sooner.

It is important to note that a congressional inquiry does not affect the SSA's final decision regarding your eligibility for disability benefits.

To request assistance from your member, contact their office and explain what government benefit you are applying for. They may ask you to submit additional documentation or complete forms through their website.

Visit MJFF's congressional directory to find your member's contact information.

ADDITIONAL RESOURCES:

ASSISTANCE FUND

The Assistance Fund's mission is to provide critically or chronically ill individuals with access to advanced therapies through a continuum of services and programs, including covering medical and prescription costs.

CONSUMER REPORTS.ORG

Consumer Reports Best Buy Drugs provides information to consumers on the costs of prescription drugs.

GOODRX.COM

This site offers prescription drug price comparisons and free coupons for consumers.

MELVIN WEINSTEIN PARKINSON'S FOUNDATION (MWPF)

MWPF offers assistance to individuals with Parkinson's disease who are struggling with financial issues to help pay for a home health aide, visiting care or to purchase specified medical equipment.

NATIONAL COUNCIL ON AGING

This organization provides a number of resources to help older adults improve their health and well being, including information on how to prevent falls.

NEEDYMEDS

This site provides information about assistance programs available to low-income patients and their advocates.

PARTNERSHIP FOR PRESCRIPTION ASSISTANCE PROGRAM

This program's mission is to increase awareness of patient assistance programs and boost enrollment of those who are eligible.

PATIENT ACCESS NETWORK FOUNDATION

This foundation provides assistance to people with Parkinson's disease who have financial need.

THE PATIENT ADVOCATE FOUNDATION

This nonprofit organization solves insurance and health care access problems by acting as a liaison between patients and insurers, employers and/or creditors.

PAYING FOR SENIOR CARE

This website is provided by The American Elder Care Research Organization to help people with Parkinson's with financial need find additional resources.

RXASSIST

RxAssist offers a comprehensive database of pharmaceutical companies' patient assistance programs and provides practical tools, news and articles.

RX OUTREACH

Rx Outreach is managed by Express Scripts Specialty Distribution Services, Inc. (ESSDS), a fully-licensed mail order pharmacy. The program offers prescription medicines to uninsured individuals and families, as well as those who have limited prescription drug coverage.

PD INFORMATION & RESOURCES

Videos – Webinars to watch, Books to read

'MY FATHER, MY BROTHER AND ME'

Frontline Documentary by Dave Iverson of PBS
video.pbs.org/video/1082086931 February, 2009-
excellent overview of PD by a person with PD.

PARKINSON'S DISEASE: A GUIDE FOR PATIENTS AND FAMILIES

From the American Academy of Neurology (2010)
Check it out at on youtube. Google: Parkinson's
Disease: A Guide for Patients and Families

Webinars Available Check these sites for lectures
on line:

PARKINSON DISEASE FOUNDATION:

http://www.pdf.org/pd_online_education
Michael J Fox Foundation- Third Thursday
Webinar or: https://www.michaeljfox.org/page.
html?hot-topics-webinar-series&navid=webinar-
series.

PARTNERS IN PARKINSONS

https://www.partnersinparkinsons.org/attend-a-
webinar

BOOKS

(Among many others)

Brainstorms, The Race to Unlock the Mysteries of Parkinson's by Jon Palfreman. Provides one with an excellent readable account of research on PD by a person living with PD.

Every Victory Counts from the Davis Phinney Foundation for Parkinson's. Essential Information and Inspiration for a Lifetime of Wellness with Parkinson's Disease. Go to the site: www.davisphinneyfoundation.org. Scroll down to Essential Tool to Living Well and click on 'order your free copy' to obtain a copy for yourself.

The New Parkinson's Disease Treatment Book, Partnering with Your Doctor to Get the Most Out of Your Medications by J Eric Ahlskog, PhD, MD from the Mayo Clinic.

A Parkinson's Primer: An Indispensable Guide to Parkinson's Disease for Patients and Their Families by John M. Vine.

Peripatetic Pursuit of Parkinson's Disease - For those with Parkinson's disease (PD), it's a support group

between two covers; and for everyone else, it's a window into the world of living with PD.
Developed by Parkinson's Creative Collective. Available to purchase through Amazon.

And, of course, *Parkinson's? You must be joking!...* by Alona Golan Sadan, Which you are reading right now…

IMPORTANT FOR PATIENTS

THE AWARE IN CARE KIT
Provided by NPF for visits to the hospital- can be
requested by calling 1-800-4PD-INFO (473-4636).
The kit includes needed info for a hospital stay.

PARKINSON'S CENTRAL APP.
A free app from NPF for people with Parkinson's
and their caregivers. www.parkinson.org/
parkinsonscentral
Partners in Parkinson's, a new resource to find
doctors, an advocate information and support-a
collaboration of Michael J Fox Foundation and
AbbVie
www.partnersinparkinsons.org

PARTNERS IN PARKINSON'S
A resource to find doctors, an advocate
information and support-a collaboration of
Michael J Fox Foundation and AbbVie **www.
partnersinparkinsons.org**

LSVT-GLOBAL
Provides information and a list of physical
therapists, occupational therapists and Speech
and Language Pathologists who are certified

to provide the special Lee Silverman Voice Treatments of LOUD and BIG that are research based programs to improve the skills of those living with PD. **www.lsvtglobal.com**

MELVIN WEINSTEIN PARKINSON'S FOUNDATION
Helping Financially Challenged Patients with PD. Phone number – 757-313-9729, website: **www.mwpf.org**, email: **mwpfassistance@verizon.net**

IMPORTANT INFO TO SHARE WITH YOUR GENERAL PHYSICIANS
Physicians Tool Kit - an app developed by National Parkinson's Foundation with detailed info on Parkinson's. Check it out yourself.
www.toolkit.parkinson.org

BE IN THE KNOW ON CURRENT RESEARCH
Medicines in Development on Parkinson's Disease – presented by America's Biopharmaceutical Research Companies - **www.phrma.org/sites/default/files/pdf/2014-parkinsons-report.pdf**

RESEARCH TO HELP THE CAUSE- TAKE PART

Michael J. Fox Foundation Trial Finder- over 77,209 are registered and watching how they can be a part. Keep in the know on current research.

foxtrialfinder.michaeljfox.org

PARKINSON ALLIANCE

Become part of research studies by completing surveys. Copies of the results will be forwarded to you. Check **www.dbs4pd.org** or 1-800-579-8440; or (609) 688-0870.

Check your local teaching hospitals with movement specialists also.

NATIONAL PARKINSON'S ORGANIZATIONS

Providing excellent Information to be shared or ordered on PD...all you need to do is ask...

AMERICAN PARKINSON'S DISEASE ASSOCIATION

135 Parkinson Ave., Staten Island, NY 10305

800-223-2732 – 718-981-8001

www.apdaparkinson.org

MICHAEL J FOX FOUNDATION
P.O. Box 4777, New York, NY 10163
800-708-7644
www.michaeljfox.org

PARKINSON'S FOUNDATION
200 SE 1st Street, Ste 800
Miami Florida 33131
800-473- 4636 1359 Broadway, Suite 1509, New York, NY 10018
Has an excellent call in Help Line 800-473- 4636
www.parkinson.org

DAVIS PHINNEY FOUNDATION
4676 Broadway, Boulder, Colorado 80304
www.davisphinneyfoundation.org 303-733-3340

LEWY BODY DEMENTIA ASSOCIATION, INC
912 Killian Hill Rd, SW,
Liburn, GA 30047
404-935-6444
www.lbda.org